PANORAMA OF WORLD ART

———

AFRICAN and OCEANIC ART

AFRICAN and

OCEANIC ART

Texts by MARGARET TROWELL

and HANS NEVERMANN

HARRY N. ABRAMS, INC. Publishers NEW YORK

End papers:

House panel with relief, Maori work from New Zealand (detail).
Museum, Auckland, New Zealand

The Art of Oceania was translated from the German
by Robert E. Wolf

Library of Congress Catalog Card Number: 68-16798

Contents

PART ONE

FORM AND CONTENT OF AFRICAN ART

TEXT BY MARGARET TROWELL

THE GEOGRAPHICAL CONDITIONS

Africa is a continent of violent contrasts, cruel yet always beautiful. From the west a belt of tropical rain forest stretches eastward along the Guinea coast and over part of the Cameroons, while farther south it covers the Gabon and northern half of the Congo. This forest is surrounded on the north, east, and south by parklike savanna fading into arid steppe and finally into complete desert in the Sahara to the north and the Kalahari to the far southwest. An area of moderately high rainfall runs down the east coast, the Nile Valley is intensively cultivated owing to its annual flooding, and the temperate conditions of the Mediterranean coast are echoed in the extreme south.

Water has always been a controlling factor as far as human settlement is concerned; for in complete desert and much of the dry steppe, man could not exist permanently, and in the denser parts of the tropical forest life was only possible in scattered clearings where small isolated groups struggled against prolific vegetation and insect-borne disease in order to eke out a primitive existence.

It is in the vast area of assured rainfall channeled by the Congo and Niger river systems that a purely African art of such consistent sculptural quality as to compel the respect of artists and connoisseurs throughout the world is to be found. To the north and along the east coast, Moslem influence has been too strong to allow the development of an African art form; while to the south, sculptural tradition hardly exists although the carving of stools, and food and milk vessels is proficient. The sculpture-producing tribes are both Negro and Bantu-speaking, and various admixtures of the two. They are chiefly agriculturalists practicing, until comparatively recently at least, the old type of agriculture, clearing their way with fire, digging sticks, and wooden hoes ever deeper into the forest, as they wore out patch after patch of worn-out cultivation. Weaker, less developed tribes had been driven further into undesirable terrain. Pygmy food-gatherers and hunters with their bows and arrows crept through almost impenetrable jungle; the bushmen went south toward the Kalahari Desert, and other more primitive people in the Western Sudan sought protection by building their huts on rocky inaccessible cliffs.

Behind the agricultural settlers came the pastoral tribes, largely Hamitic. These people, certainly no less intelligent than the agriculturalists over whom they usually claimed overlordship, preferred the nomadic life, leading their cattle seasonally from one area to another in search of water. Such a life did not encourage the accumulation of material possessions, and sculpture is not found among them.

An African people in migration sought a country richer than that from which they had come, an environment in which their particular way of life might be fully developed, whether it was agricultural, mixed farming, or purely pastoral. Having once settled, they were completely dependent on their environment not only for food but also for all the materials they needed for building, clothing, and all other necessities. Fertile soil and sufficient water supply were the first requisites, then the wherewithal to build.

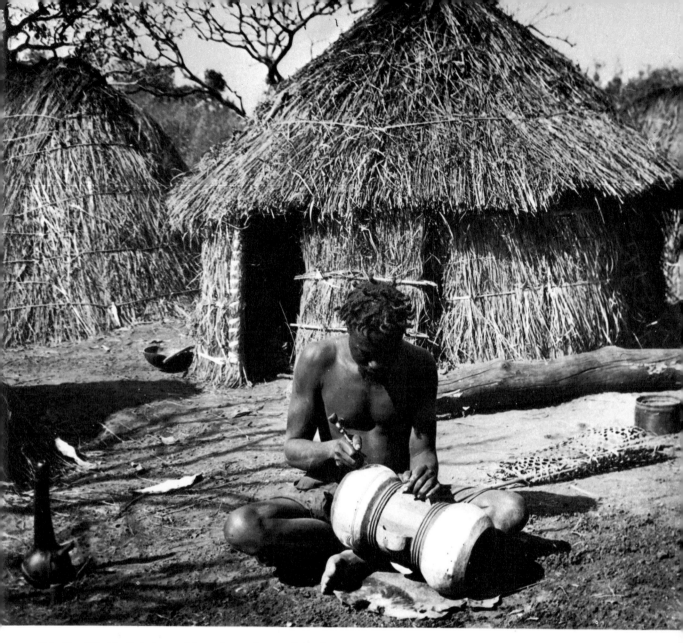

Primitive "Beehive" shelter on left, and grass hut on right. Congo

BASIC MATERIALS AND THEIR USES

Stone was not much used for building, for good quality stone of the right type is rare in Africa, although in Zimbabwe in Rhodesia great blocks of local granite were used. Softer stone was used for carving in certain places on the Sierra Leone–Liberian border, in Yorubaland, and in the Lower Congo. The firing of bricks

7

Village in arid savanna country. Banchi Province. Northern Nigeria

does not seem to have been indigenous, but mud or clay was used in some places beaten into solid walls. The more usual type of hut building throughout most of the country was of interlaced sticks covered with clay or

Seminomadic Hima with their herds. Uganda

mud and roofed with some sort of thatch. Such buildings could not be expected to last for more than a few years and could scarcely be termed architecture. Great palaces of almost mythical splendor were in existence, however, in Benin and Dahomey in the last century; but now they have gone, and we can only turn to the writings of some of the early explorers for records of their grandeur.

Wood was ubiquitous and all-important, both the hardwoods of the forests and the soft, lighter woods of the open parklands. For building, the Africans cut poles, they split trunks into rough planks, they set up hurdle walls of sticks and canes, tied them with thongs of twisted bark and daubed them over with sticky mud. They set poles as rafters from a central post to the circular wall and thatched with papyrus, rush, reeds, grass, or palm branches. They carved logs into milk pots and food vessels, into stools and headrests. They hollowed out trunks into canoes and made doors for their huts and granaries out of thick planks. They carved ritual figures and masks for religious ceremonies.

Second in importance to wood were the canes and fibers from sisal-like plants, creepers from the forests, palms, reeds, and so forth, which were not only used for thatching but also stripped, split, soaked, and woven

9

or plaited into ropes, clothes, and mats, or fish traps and baskets of many kinds. This was largely a woman's craft, which girls learned from their mothers while still young children.

Hides were to the pastoralists what fibers were to the farming folk. They flung them round their bodies as cloaks, shredded and twisted them for thongs, sewed them into buckets, bags, sacks, and rough tents. They even dampened the inner skin and fitted it over a clay mold until it dried out perfectly shaped as a water bottle.

Pottery was usually a woman's craft. Water pots and cooking vessels were coiled and roughly fired, and in certain tribes higher quality polished and decorated pots were made, chiefly by men. Life-sized terra-cotta figures were made at Nok in northern Nigeria over two thousand years ago, and others at Ife perhaps a thousand years later.

Iron has been found in the Nok cultural deposits, and thus may be assumed to have been worked in Africa since very early days. The smith has always been regarded with awe and his craft surrounded by a mass of taboos and superstitions. Bronze and brass casting has been practiced among a number of the Guinea coast tribes, most outstandingly in the kingdoms of Ife, Benin, and Ashanti.

THE CRAFTSMAN'S APPROACH

While the women practiced their crafts on their own doorsteps, the men, with their more specialized trades, worked together in little potteries or carvers' workshops, which were family or clan affairs. Sometimes a boy or two would be helping the father or older relative in the compound, or sometimes, as in the workshops of the greater chiefs or royal courts, a system of formal apprenticeship might exist.

The handing on of cultural traditions in these small, family workshops, combined with the isolation imposed by difficulties of communication with the outside world, led to great conservatism. Thus and thus had a stool always been carved or a figure of a woman always shaped, and the craftsman conformed to the generic patterns as his patrons and fellow tribesmen expected him to do. Moreover, it was not only the living tribal patrons

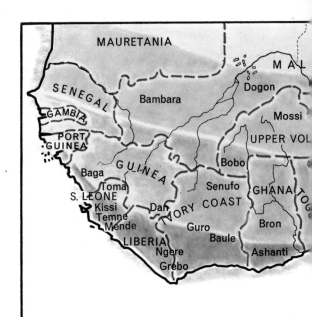

The Tribes and Climatic Zones of Africa

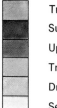

Tropical rain forest

Subtropical forest

Upland savanna and forest

Tropical savanna

Dry grassland

Semidesert and desert

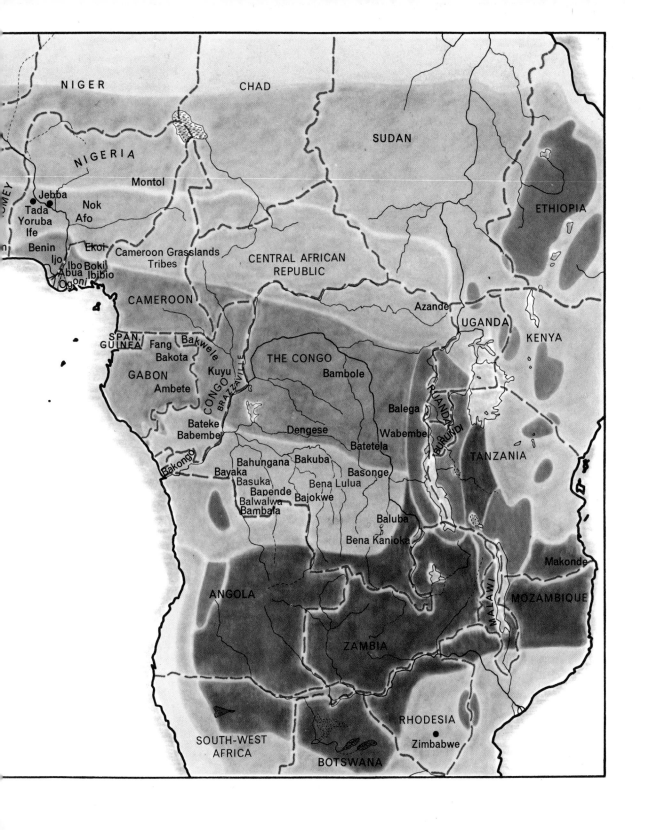

NIGER

CHAD

NIGERIA

SUDAN

ETHIOPIA

Montol

Jebba
DOMEY
Tada
Yoruba
Ife

Nok
Afo

Benin
Ijo
Ekoi
Cameroon Grasslands
Tribes

CENTRAL AFRICAN
REPUBLIC

Ibo Bokii
Abua Ibibio
Ogoni

CAMEROON

Azande

UGANDA

KENYA

SPAN.
GUINEA
Fang
Bakwele

Bakota

THE CONGO

Bambole

GABON

Kuyu

Ambete

CONGO
BRAZZAVILLE

Balega

RUANDA

Bateke
Babembe

Dengese

Wabembe

BURUNDI

TANZANIA

Batetela

Bakongo

Bahungana
Bakuba

Basonge

Bayaka
Basuka
Bapende
Bena Lulua
Balwalwa
Bajokwe
Bambala

Baluba

Bena Kanioka

Makonde

ANGOLA

MALAWI

MOZAMBIQUE

ZAMBIA

RHODESIA

Zimbabwe

SOUTH-WEST
AFRICA

BOTSWANA

Huts with decorated doorways. Ghana

whose approval was necessary. There were the spirits of the ancestors, the spirit of the tree from which the wood had been taken, and the spirits whose aid would be sought in the rituals for which the carving was being prepared. Only by absolute conformity with past tradition and by making the accustomed rites and sacrifices could the craftsman be assured of their approval.

COURT ART

We have spoken of migrations sweeping across the land and forcing tribes into less desirable areas, or in some cases settling alongside as their overlords. This was not necessarily a case of military conquest. But the Western Sudan to the north of the sculpture-making tribes of the Upper Volta and the Guinea coast was, in

Building a pot

Final carving of a mask

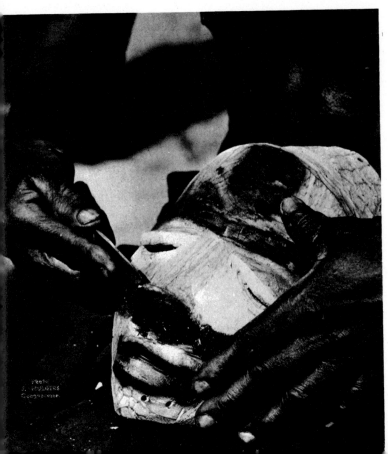

the Middle Ages, the site of a number of great empires both Moslem and pagan, built up by military force. It was also a center of learning, with a Moslem university at Timbuktu, and the influence of these kingdoms filtered southward. As far as sculpture was concerned, Moslem influence was merely negative, for their religion forbade the making of graven images. But highly developed kingdoms sprang up farther south. The Ashanti of the Gold Coast (now Ghana) were at the height of their power in the seventeenth century. The neighboring territories of Togoland and Dahomey also had their

Stool carvers working with adzes

ruling sovereigns, while in Nigeria Ife and the Benin were the most famous kingdoms of them all. The rulers of these kingdoms were all-powerful within their states. They employed their own royal craftsmen, highly skilled in every art, who could work for no one else. The craftsmen carved "tusks with mythological and historical designs installed on the altars of the king's ancestors" (Benin); gongs were "struck at court to signify the king's approval" (Benin) and "images modeled to commemorate deceased members of the royal or privileged families" (Krinjabo). In the Cameroons some kings and greater chiefs also received the same sort of homage; while in the central Congo the Bakuba claim that their kingdom dates back to the sixteenth century, and nineteen portrait statues of their kings, not all contemporaneous, exist today.

As well as ceremonial sculpture made for the kings alone, there were in all these kingdoms artifacts of every kind—bowls, stools, textiles, musical instruments, and pottery—made with a care and sophisticated expertise with which the carver of the more democratic tribes made no attempt to compete. It was, in fact, a "court art," refined and polished but often insensitive and somewhat lacking in real aesthetic value. It might well be called "man-regarding art," for it aimed at pleasing the patron, be he mighty king or petty chief. Such work, splendid as it is in many respects, does not bring out the finest qualities in African sculpture.

Basket making. Kiga. Western Uganda

RELIGIOUS BELIEFS AND RITUAL OBJECTS

These deeper aesthetic qualities are found more often in sculpture which is concerned with African ritual and belief—carvings which are often at once less highly finished and far more powerful than "court" or "man-regarding" art. We might, using the same terminology, call it "spirit-regarding" art. Just what this involves is difficult for a European or even the young African of the present day to comprehend.

If we are to attempt to understand the beliefs of the African of the old world—and we must make this attempt if we are to have a sensitive appreciation of his sculpture—we must first put on one side our own prevailing conception of each individual as a unique personal being encased within the shell of his own body, influenced only to a limited degree by communication with other unique personalities, and replace it by the concept of selfhood "spilling out into the world beyond the confines of the experiencing body and echoing back again from other selves ... interpermeating other selves in a relationship in which subject and object are no longer distinguishable." (J.V.Taylor, *The Primal Vision,* London, 1963, p. 45.)

15

This sense of a fluid spiritual force coursing through mankind was limited only by the Africans' knowledge of the outer world. Where travel and communication were difficult, it was virtually confined to the family, clan, and tribe, together with neighboring tribal enemies whose spirits were greatly to be feared. This must have accounted for the tremendously strong ties of loyalty between blood relations, clan brothers, and tribesmen. They were literally "one people," and the individual was only one small fragment of the fluctuating life of the tribe.

But this sense of oneness, of participation in the spirit, went even beyond the boundary of mankind. It included participation in the whole visible and invisible universe; the dead were still an intrinsic and powerful part of the family; indeed, in matters of the spirit they were more powerful than the living themselves. Furthermore, not only the living and the dead but also other forms of existence—the very rocks and stones, and, in fact, the whole cosmos—were included in the Africans' conception of this unified totality which they sought to participate in and to apprehend. The visible and invisible world, the human and divine, the past and present, formed one harmonious whole, and man had to fit himself into this unity. Taboos must not be violated, rites of passage and other rituals must be observed, spirits must be appeased, and above all, the power, life force, or mana (the driving force of all existence) must be enticed, placated, and harnessed for the well-being of the tribe or smaller groups within it.

It is dangerous to dogmatize on a subject about which so little is yet known or to generalize concerning the beliefs of so many different tribes, but it would seem that most Africans acknowledge a creator—far off and not particularly concerned with his creation. Then for each tribe there is a pantheon of lesser gods and spirits—thunder gods, earth goddesses, spirits of plague, fire, and water; mythical original ancestors of the tribe; and more recent ancestors still personally remembered. There are societies and cults the purpose of which is to insure, through ritual acts, the increase of the tribe, its cattle, and its crops. The members of these societies hold dances and ceremonies at appropriate times to accomplish this end. The greater part of African sculpture is connected with this necessity.

The sculpture illustrated in this book has been chosen to give some idea of the kind of work which spiritual and practical needs called forth in the old African world and of its great variety and high aesthetic value. This older traditional sculpture must be considered as the classical period of African art. We may find it difficult to understand because it speaks in the foreign language of a foreign culture, but its aesthetic quality is clear for all to see. It is often expressionistic, but that is but one quality of African art and one which has special pitfalls for the unwary stranger. Only too often do we read into a work of art our own psychological reactions and afford it an interpretation which its maker would never consciously have striven to communicate.

It is all important to remember that African sculpture is not designed to convey to the onlooker the character of the spiritual powers. The sculptures are ritual objects made to be used in ritual acts, aimed to influence not the human beholder but the spiritual powers themselves. They are channels through which the life force may enter this temporal world and influence it. For this purpose four main categories of ritual sculpture may be recognized—the mask, the ancestor or cult figure, the fetish, and the reliquary. These are placed first in this book because they are of prime and more general importance. Then follow the works of the historic kingdoms where wealth and prestige developed a court art; and finally, some of the artifacts, such as pottery and textiles, which were found not only in the palaces of the kings and greater chiefs but also among the people of the more developed tribes.

By arranging the illustrations according to their subject matter, we have deliberately abandoned the normal practice of ordering them by tribes. This layout actually has the advantage of making the differences between tribal styles more dramatic, and a rapid glance at caption and map should make clear to the reader the provenance of each piece.

Nimba mask. Baga. Guinea. Wood with fiber cape, height of head 23¼″. The British Museum, London

MASKS, FIGURES, AND FETISHES

Although as we have said we must strive not to read our own reactions into an expressionistic work of another culture knowing nothing of its psychological background, we should nevertheless, having found out all that we can about the piece, be prepared to throw ourselves open to receive its impact.

This great carving, of which the head alone is over twenty-three inches high, is one of the most monumental sculptures conceivable. The features are near human in form, but transcendent, impassive, and inscrutable.

Nimba personifies fertility, and on the fertility of crops, livestock, and the tribe itself all life depends. For this reason, before the rice is harvested, Nimba appears from the bush (raised on the shoulders of its carrier, who is hidden by the long fiber cape) and leads the village to celebrate in solemn ceremonial dance.

Figure used in the cure of sickness. Montol. Nigeria. Wood, height 15³/₄″. Collection Wielgus, Chicago

From Nimba the incomprehensible we turn to this little human figure, yearning and straining intensely upward. Its purpose was to obtain the cure of sickness, and in no other work of art can this ever-present need for supernatural aid have been more movingly yet unsentimentally portrayed.

Fetish figure. Basonge. Congo. Wood,
fiber, feathers, beads, etc. The British
Museum, London

Grim and dour is this fetish—evil, malignant, and cruel. Its stomach is packed with the malevolent ingredients of power—blood, bile, excrement, and so forth—a veritable witch's potion. Its face appears as hard as the wood from which it was carved.

DANCING AND THE MASK

African ideology is largely manifested in cults which aim to increase the life force of the tribal community, together with that of the crops, the cattle, and the game upon which it depends. One of the chief methods of accomplishing this is through the ritual dance, and the chief appurtenance of the dance is the mask.

Dances are held during funerary rites for members of tribal societies; at annual celebrations for the dead; and at other times and seasons, too, such as during various rites of passage, when the spiritual forces are particularly potent and call for propitiatory action. The dance is central in agrarian ceremonies. In these performances animal masks may be worn. Through their use and the miming actions which accompany them, the whole saga of the primitive search for the control of the forces of nature connected with hunting, cultivation, and animal husbandry, on which the tribe depends for its very existence, is played out.

Dance after the young girls' initiation ceremony. The paint is generally applied after excision. Ngere. Toulepleu region, Ivory Coast

Dance mask for the yam cult. Ibo. Nigeria. Wood

Dancing is believed to increase the power of the performers themselves. More important, however, is that it is the expression of the Africans' strong sense of unity with the spiritual world. The departed elders of the tribe are considered to be sharing in the performance and acting as powerful intermediaries or channels of power. When a man wears a mask in honor of a particular spirit, he is no longer himself but has temporarily become that spirit.

Masks are based on human or animal forms or often a mixture of both. Sometimes they are completely naturalistic, and often idealized; sometimes formalized and abstract. It is generally possible to judge fairly accurately the area from which a mask has come, for each tribe or subtribe has developed its own conventions according to its own predilections and traditions. Masks are worn not only in front of the face; they may be worn horizontally on the top of the head or tipped diagonally on the forehead. Some masks fit over the head like a helmet, and tall headdresses are worn attached to a tight-fitting cap of basketwork.

Dance headdress. Abua. Lower Oraski River. Nigeria.
Wood, fibers, etc.

Masked dancers. Bapende. Congo

Some masks are deliberately terrifying and are used to scare away strangers, especially women, from initiation rites and other ceremonies of the various "secret" societies. These Bapende masked figures, for instance, keep the women away from tribal puberty rites. In some regions, notably among the Ibibio and Ekoi, the Ekpo society was all-powerful, seeking not only to propitiate the ancestors but also to control the living community through terrorization, and its masks were macabre, aggressive, and horrifying.

This is a splendid example of the Senufo style of formalization. The highly polished, convex oval head has a clearly defined, concave, heart-shaped facial area and a long, thin nose with strongly accentuated nostrils. Various horns and side-pieces have been added which, together with certain areas of the face, are decorated with crosshatched pattern. On each side of the chin, the typical Senufo "legs" hang downward.

Mask. Senufo. Ivory Coast. Wood and fibers, etc., height 14^1/$_8$". The Museum of Primitive Art, New York

Mask. Bapende. Congo. Wood and fibers, height $12^1/_4''$. The Allen Memorial Art Museum, Oberlin, Ohio

The equally beautiful but very naturalistic mask on this page stands in complete contrast with the last one. A typical Bapende feature of the work is the sharply cut nose.

Notice how the fiber wigs and capes greatly enhance the appearance of these two masks. (Unfortunately, the fiber hangings of many masks are missing when the specimens reach the museums.)

This elegant mask from a subtribe of the Senufo has so much high relief detail that it rather detracts from the basic form of the face. Doubtless it would hold together better as a solid unit when surrounded by the massive wig-cape which would be worn with it during the dance.

Mask worn at puberty ceremonies. Makonde. Tanzania-Mozambique border. Wood, height 13³/₄". Lindenmuseum, Stuttgart

This excellent mask shows again the delight taken by African sculptors among tribes stretching from the Fang, through the Bakota, Bakwele, and Balega right across Africa, in the heart-shaped face with the strong vertical ridge of the nose supporting the curves of the brows.

Female Mask. Bajokwe. Congo. Wood, height 9½″. Musée de la Vie Indigène, Leopoldville

Male Mask. Bajokwe. Congo. Wood, height 9⅞″. Musée Royal de l'Afrique Centrale, Tervueren, Belgium

Much of the sculpture of the Bajokwe strikes us at first glance as ugly and repulsive. Yet the first of these two masks has a wonderful depth and serenity which few carvings can equal.

In strong contrast is the second mask, which shows the more usual characteristics of the tribal sculpture. It is a male head to which the curving lines of the brow and cheekbones give a curious bespectacled effect. The great open mouth with its serrated teeth completes the ferocious appearance of the mask. Similar pairs of "beauty and the beast" masks, now worn at village entertainments, may at one time have been used in initiation rites.

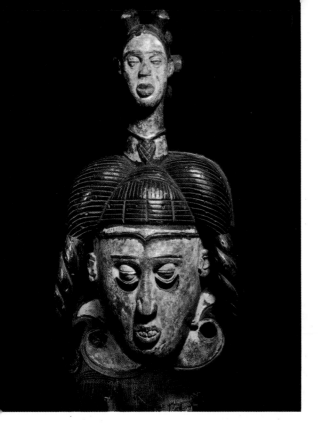

The Ibibio and Baule masks are good representative specimens of the work of their respective tribes; the Baule features, as usual, are more refined, although the two top masks are very similar in form. The Bambara mask is more rare, and through its extreme simplification achieves great dignity.

Dance mask. Ibibio. Nigeria. Wood, height 22$^{1}/_{2}$".
The Museum of Primitive Art, New York

Dance mask. Baule. Ivory Coast. Wood, height 11".
Collection Kamer, Cannes

Dance mask. Baule. Ivory Coast. Wood, height 16¹/₂″. Collection ▶
Maurice Nicaud, Paris

Dance mask. Bambara. Mali. Wood, height 11³/₈″.
Collection Kamer, Cannes

31

Gelede society mask. Yoruba. Nigeria. Wood, height
16$^1\!/_2''$. Jos Museum, Nigeria

Mask. Dan. Ivory Coast–Liberia border. Wood, height 11″. Collection Morris Pinto, Paris

The Yoruba mask, carved nearly a hundred years ago, is a very vigorous, sharply defined, naturalistic head. A beautiful piece of work carved with much understanding of form, it is worn flat on the top of the dancer's head at the yearly festivals and funeral ceremonies of members of the Gelede society, an increase cult of the southwestern Yoruba.

The Dan mask is also very naturalistic, but it has as well a moving quality which is difficult to define. It is poetry whereas the other is first-class prose.

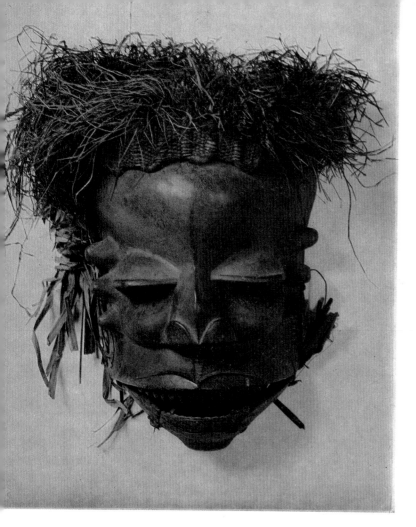

Ekpo society mask worn at the yam harvest ceremonies. Ibibio. Nigeria. Wood, height 13³/₄″. Lindenmuseum, Stuttgart

This fine mask belongs to the Ekpo society, chief increase society of the Ibibio tribe, which also functions to keep order among the people.

The crisply cut lines of the lips, nostrils, cheekbones, and eyes give a lovely rhythm to the head. The lower jaw is hinged and mobile.

The heavy, solid Mende helmet mask on the opposite page has none of the attractive grace of the Ekpo society mask, but has, nevertheless, very interesting formal qualities. It is basically a cone, which is emphasized by the upsweeping curve of the brow. The whole frontal area is divided into two strongly differentiated triangles, brow and face. It is worn with a large fiber cape hanging from the base.

Ekkpe society mask worn at festivals and funeral ▶
ceremonies of members. Ekoi. Nigeria. Wood covered
with antelope skin, height 11″. The Museum of Primitive Art, New York

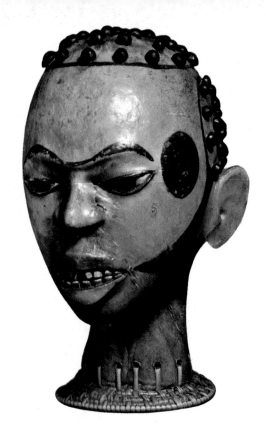

Women's Bundu society mask worn by officials at
initiation ceremonies. Mende. Sierra Leone. Wood,
height 15³/₄″. The British Museum, London. Plass
Collection

The Ekkpe society is an increase cult of the Ekoi. These
skin-covered masks are striking for their realism rather
than for their formal qualities. Talbot recorded, in
1926, that after battle, Ekoi warriors danced a victory
celebration with the heads of their slain enemies tied
on their own heads. These masks may have originated
as substitutes, which would account for their extreme
naturalism.

Crested mask of the Mmwo society (cult of female ancestral spirits). Ibo. Nigeria. Wood, height
15³/₄″. The British Museum, London

Here are three white-faced masks from the Ibo and Ogoni. The first is a helmet mask with a thin, high crest
running from back to front, finely carved and decorated. The features are stylized and refined in the carving
so that the general appearance is thin and sharp. The masks are worn with brilliant red and yellow tight-
fitting costumes at festivals and funeral ceremonies of the society. The second mask from the Ibo of Orlu is
a face mask, altogether more solid in appearance and with interesting facial decoration in heavy black.

Mask worn in the Okorosia play. Ibo of Orlu. Nigeria. Wood, height 10⅝″. The Liverpool Museum

Elu mask. Ogoni. Nigeria. Wood, height 7⅞″. The Liverpool Museum

The third mask, from the Ogoni tribe, is a very striking piece. It has a hinged lower jaw, which the wearer manipulates with his mouth so that it opens and shuts noisily. These masks are worn by members of societies based on age groups at various social events.

Dance mask. Bayaka. Congo. Wood with fibers, height 16$\frac{1}{8}$″. Musée Royal de l'Afrique Centrale, Tervueren, Belgium

Bayaka masks, often highly grotesque and brightly colored, with large fiber capes, are worn by the young initiates as they return dancing to their villages after the circumcision ceremonies are over.

Mask. Bafo. Cameroons. Wood, height $12^5/_8''$.
Museum für Völkerkunde, Berlin

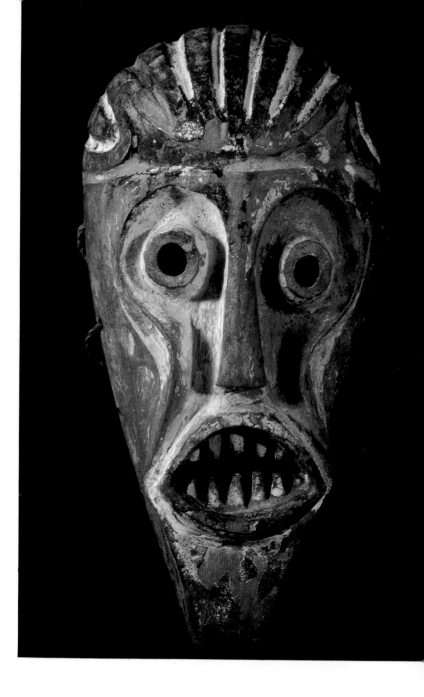

This mask and the following ones are highly stylized. This long-faced one combines a heart-shaped facial plane with circular eyes and an oval mouth decorated with serrated teeth. It is fiercely expressionistic.

Mask. Abua. Congo. Wood, height 12¹/₄″. Musée Royal de l'Afrique Centrale, Tervueren, Belgium

In the top mask, a completely cubist pattern has been developed from the planes of the forehead, eye sockets, nose, cheek, and mouth areas and from the decorative use of the circular ears.

The bottom mask is more naturalistic, but the simplified forms of the face, mouth, and salient nose give it an aggressive appearance expressionistically treated.

Mask used at dances after circumcision. Balwalwa. Congo. Wood, height 14¹/₈″. Musée Royal de l'Afrique Centrale, Tervueren, Belgium

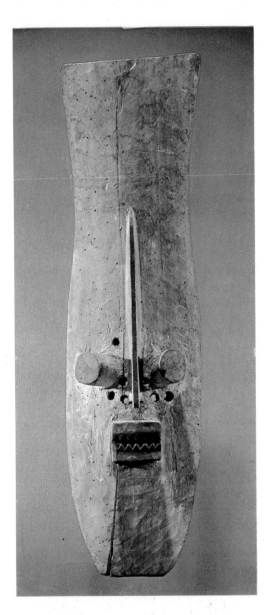

Here are two masks shorn of all irrelevant detail, which stand in complete contrast with one another. The Grebo is abstract, expressionistic, and aggressive; the Guro shows sensitive delight in modulated and gently flowing form.

Mask. Grebo. Ngere complex of tribes. Liberia. Wood, height 27⅝″. The Museum of Primitive Art, New York

Mask. Guro. Ivory Coast. Wood, height 17¾″. The Museum of Primitive Art, New York

Mask. Bena Kanioka. Congo. Wood, height 11³/₈″. Hamburgisches Museum für Völkerkunde und Vorgeschichte, Hamburg

Head. Balega. Congo. Ivory, height 5¹/₂″. Collection Charles Ratton, Paris

These round-faced masks and head are all approached in interesting ways.

The Bena Kanioka translates the face into a number of harmonious geometrical forms; the Balega and Baule reduce the form to complete simplicity. The Baluba, while keeping the actual form as simple as possible, strongly emphasizes its rhythm through the use of concentric circles.

▲

Mask for the Goli dance to avert misfortune. Baule. Ivory Coast. Wood, height 39″. Collection Duperrier, Paris

Mask for the Goli dance to avert misfortune. Baule. Ivory Coast. Wood, height 33½″. Collection Pierre Vérité, Paris

◀ Kifwebe mask used by witch doctors. Baluba. Congo. Wood, height 14⅝″. The Museum of Primitive Art, New York

We have already noted the heart-shaped face, which in these examples is even more clearly defined. Perhaps the simplest and most beautiful is the Fang; white, delicately outlined in black, it presents an uncanny, ghostly appearance.

Ngi society mask worn by members when detecting and punishing sorcerers. Fang. Gabon. Wood, height 25⅝″. Collection Withof, Brussels

Dance mask. Baule. Ivory Coast. Wood, height 12⅝″. Musée des Arts Africains et Océaniens, Paris

Dance mask. Bakwele. Congo (Brazzaville). Wood, height 21¼". The Museum of Primitive Art, New York

In this Bakwele mask the heart shape is not formed by the face but by the downward-curving horns.

Dance mask. Bakwele. Congo (Brazzaville). Wood,
height 11³/₈″. Musée des Arts Africains et Océaniens,
Paris

Here rejection of all irrelevant detail has produced a simple, abstract mask of very great beauty. The work
on the next page crowns an almost identical form with a curious superstructure.

The work of this tribe has the same indefinable sensitivity and beauty as that of certain other tribes in the northern half of the Congo, such as the Fang to the west and the Bambole and Balega to the east. Should we call it expressionistic? It is dangerous to use our own terminology when we know so little of the mental and emotional background of the makers of these masks, but that would seem the most appropriate term from our Western art vocabulary.

Dance mask. Bakwele. Congo (Brazzaville). Wood, height 24". Musée d'Histoire Naturelle, La Rochelle, France

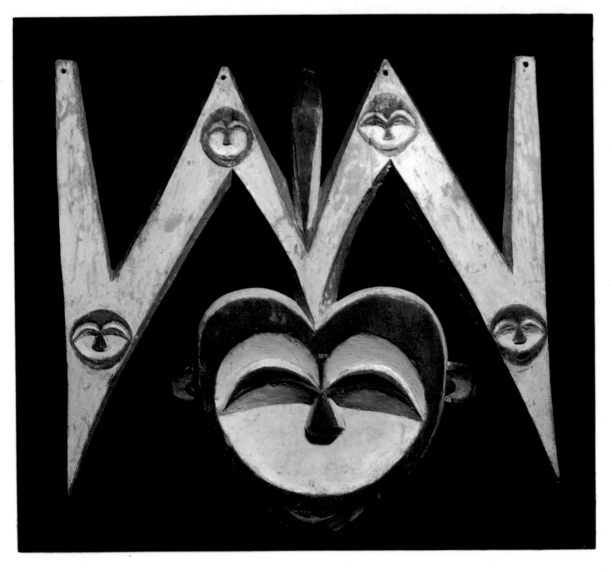

Mask. Bateke. Congo (Brazzaville). Wood, height 13³/₄". Musée de l'Homme, Paris

These two abstract masks are not completely nonrepresentational, for in both the "idea" of eyes and nose is clearly to be seen. These features have been abstracted from the basic scheme of a human face and used as the foundation for a formal pattern. The resulting Bateke mask is more attractive, but the larger mask on the right is more powerful and impressive. It belongs to a men's society and represents the spirit of the bush.

Dance mask. Wabembe. Congo. Wood, height without feathers $18^1/_8''$.
Musée Royal de l'Afrique Centrale, Tervueren, Belgium

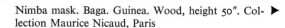
Nimba mask. Baga. Guinea. Wood, height 50″. Collection Maurice Nicaud, Paris ▶

◀ Dance mask used in rites to expel the souls of the recently dead. Dogon. Mali. Wood, height 14⁵/₈″. Musée de l'Homme, Paris

Mask of the Poro society. Toma. Guinea Coast. Wood, height 22¹/₂″. Musée de la Ville, Angoulême, France

These three large masks are all held in great awe for their spiritual power.

The Dogon, wearing this mask, try to break all ties with the spiteful spirits of those who died in anger with their relatives and who are still dangerous to the community.

The Toma mask belongs to the all-powerful and feared political Poro society.

Nimba is the great fertility figure of the Baga tribe, feared, respected, and invoked by all.

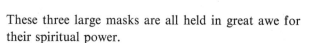

Dance mask. Bamum. Cameroon Grasslands. Wood,
height 33$^{1}/_{2}$". The British Museum, London
▼

In contrast with the previous set of masks, these
four from the Cameroon Grasslands are richly
comic; indeed, they are mostly used for entertain-
ment, in stilt dances and the like.

Dance mask. Bacham. Cameroon Grasslands. Wood, height 26³/₈″. Rietberg Museum, Zurich

Dance mask. Bafum. Cameroon Grasslands. Wood, height 11³/₄″. Collection Tristan Tzara, Paris

For craftsmanship, the Bacham mask, with its cubistic division of the face into well-defined planes, and the Bafum, with the sculptural quality of its roughly adzed surface, are outstanding.

53

◀ Dance mask. Bakuba. Congo. Wood, height 9½″. The British Museum, London

Helmet mask. Bakuba. Congo. Wood and antelope skin. Musée Royal de l'Afrique Centrale, Tervueren, Belgium

Kifwebe mask, used by witch doctors. Basonge. Congo. Wood, height 14⅛″. Collection Kamer, Cannes
▼

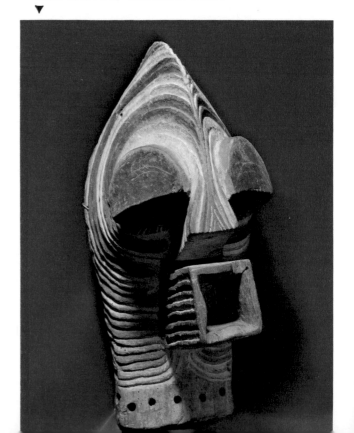

In each of these masks the three-dimensional form is strongly emphasized by the colored surface pattern.

Kifwebe mask. Basonge. Congo. Wood, height 15″. Musée Royal de l'Afrique Centrale, Tervueren, Belgium

Dance mask. Batetela. Congo. Wood, height excluding cape and horns 18¹/₈″. The British Museum, London ▶

◀ Dance mask. Bakuba. Congo. Wood, fiber, cowries, and beads, height 13″. Musée Royal de l'Afrique Centrale, Tervueren, Belgium

Dance mask. Bakuba. Congo. Wood, fiber, cowries, and beads, height 20⅛″. Musée Royal de l'Afrique Centrale, Tervueren, Belgium

As in the masks on the two previous pages, these masks belong to a tribe in whose work color and surface pattern are as important as the underlying form and are always in complete accord with it. The Bakuba, or Bushongo as they are sometimes called, are renowned for their decorative carving of wooden cups, boxes, and other vessels, as well as for their woven and embroidered cloth.

Ekpo society mask. Ibibio. Nigeria. Wood, leather, and fibers, height 7⅞". Museum of Archaeology and Ethnology, Cambridge, England

DEFORMITY MASKS

Certain African masks, notably those of the powerful Ekpo society of the Ibibio, are deliberately macabre. This one, with its blackened skull-like form and enormous flapping ears of hide, appears horrific when worn. The next, a terrible reminder of the deformities caused by yaws, is the more horrible because of its stark realism. Such sights were only too common in Africa.

Ekpo society mask.
Ibibio. Nigeria. Wood,
height 13³/₄″. The British
Museum, London

Mask. Ngere-Wobe. Ivory Coast–Liberia border. Wood, height 8¼″. Collection Kamer, Cannes

▲
Mask. Ogoni. Nigeria. Wood, height 7⅞″. The Museum of Primitive Art, New York. Leff Collection

Of these three masks, the first, from the Ivory Coast–Liberia border, is very naturalistic and appears to represent the results of disease. The other two are rather abstract suggestions of deformity.

Ekpo society mask. Ibibio. Nigeria. Wood, height 12⅝″. The Baltimore Museum of Art

Janiform headdress mask. Ekoi. Nigeria. Wood and antelope skin, height 15³/₄″. The British Museum, London

Janiform headdress mask. Boki. Nigeria. Wood, height 10¼". Collection Charles Ratton, Paris

JANUS-HEADED MASKS

The Janiform Ekoi mask belongs to the Ekpo society, a cult of the ancestor spirits. It is made even more realistic by the covering of the wooden form with antelope skin. The neighboring Boki carve masks which are similar in style but do not have the skin covering. This particular one has an expressionistic appeal which is lacking in the more static Ekoi heads.

Janiform dance mask. Baule. Ivory Coast. Wood, height 11³/₄″. Collection Pierre Vérité, Paris

Janiform dance mask. Guro. Ivory Coast. Wood, height 15″. Collection Pierre Vérité, Paris

The Baule, Guro, and Senufo tribes of the Ivory Coast also used Janiform masks. The Baule mask, on the left, is a beautiful piece of sculpture, quietly statuesque. On the right, the Guro mask with its two heads, one antelope and the other human, is lively and full of character.

Dance mask. Ngere. Liberia. Wood; ▶
orange, blue, and white paint; red fabric;
tin; cotton cord; fiber; cloth and woolen
ornaments; nails; and cartridge cases,
height 13″. The Museum of Primitive Art,
New York

Dance mask. Ngere. Liberia. Wood, height 13³/₈″. Collection Eliot
Elisofon, New York

THE WARTHOG MASKS OF THE NGERE TRIBES

The wart-hog masks of the Ngere are among the most aggressively exciting works of African art. Even a list
of all the materials used in one construction makes a colorful assemblage, as is shown by the caption of the
mask on the opposite page.

Dance mask. Ngere. Liberia. Wood, coloring matter, metal, fiber, cloth, height 13³/₈″. The Museum of Primitive Art, New York. Leff Collection

Neither animal nor human, these masks are given certain abstract forms—cylinders, horns, large salient noses, deep-lipped mouths with prominent teeth—all in rich profusion.

Dance mask. Dan-Ngere complex of tribes. Liberia. Wood, height 12⅝″. National Museum, Copenhagen

This mask from the Dan-Ngere complex of tribes, although belonging to the wart-hog type of mask, has replaced the fiercely aggressive appearance by a strong but harmonious three-dimensional pattern of curving horns.

Of the large collection of tribes making up this complex group, it is the Ngere whose masks are noted as dominantly cubistic and grotesque. Those of the Dan are the least distorted and some are extremely naturalistic.

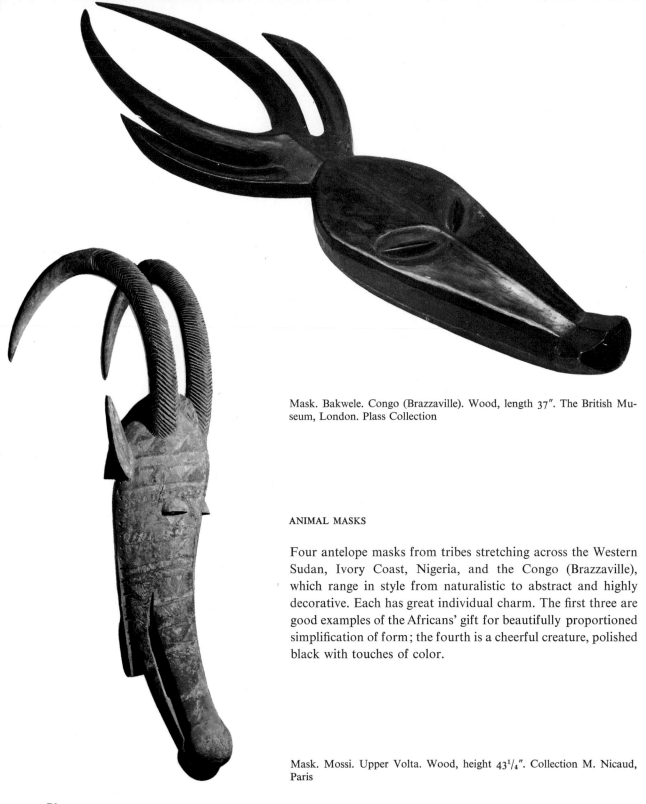

Mask. Bakwele. Congo (Brazzaville). Wood, length 37″. The British Museum, London. Plass Collection

ANIMAL MASKS

Four antelope masks from tribes stretching across the Western Sudan, Ivory Coast, Nigeria, and the Congo (Brazzaville), which range in style from naturalistic to abstract and highly decorative. Each has great individual charm. The first three are good examples of the Africans' gift for beautifully proportioned simplification of form; the fourth is a cheerful creature, polished black with touches of color.

Mask. Mossi. Upper Volta. Wood, height 43¹/₄″. Collection M. Nicaud, Paris

◀ Karikpo mask. Ogoni. Southern Nigeria. Wood, height 17³/₈″. Collection Kenneth Murray, Lagos

Zamle society mask. Guro. Ivory Coast. Wood. The British Museum, London. Plass Collection ▼

All these masks are probably used in dancing at the farming festivals. The Ogoni mask is said to dedicate the farming season to the local deity. The Guro is the mask of the Zamle society which produces antelope dances to ensure increase of the crops.

Korubla mask for an anti-sorcery society. Senufo. Ivory Coast. Wood, height 35⅞". Musée de l'Homme, Paris

The Senufo helmet masks *(korubla)* are called "fire-spitters" because the mouths are stuffed with burning tinder. They are worn on the top of the head. This one shows a mixture of human and animal features, and has a chameleon and a bird between the horns. It is an exciting but complicated design.

The Bali elephant, on the other hand, is to be noted for its great simplicity of form.

The Ekoi headdress mask, with its fantastic widespread mouth, is in grotesque contrast to the naturalistic human masks of the same tribe shown earlier in this book.

◀ Mask. Bali. Cameroon Grasslands. Wood, height 28″. The British Museum, London

Mask. Ekoi. Nigeria. Wood, covered with skin, length 15″. Museum für Völkerkunde, Berlin

Chi wara dance headdress. Bambari. Mali. Wood, ▶
height 16¹/₈″. National Museum, Copenhagen

THE ANTELOPE HEADDRESSES OF THE BAMBARA

A mythical being called Chi wara is tradition-
ally believed to have taught the Bambara to
cultivate grain, and the young men dance in
his honor after hoeing contests during the
planting season.

The antelope headdresses which they wear
fixed on their heads by basketwork caps
covered with fiber capes are quite outstanding
as works of three-dimensional design. They
are of light wood, usually between twenty-four
and twenty-eight inches high, and are seen to
their best advantage in the movement of the
dance.

They range from the extreme naturalism
of the one on the left, which appears to be
peering nervously through the long grass, to
the beautifully rhythmic abstract pattern of
the one on the right.

Chi wara dance headdress. Bambara. Mali. Wood,
height 21¹/₄″. Formerly Collection Rubinstein, Paris

These two headdresses are centered on a vertical axis. The first is rigid and sharply and squarely cut; the second balances its arabesque of curving mane against the more simple flattened arc of the horns and head.

Chi wara dance headdress. Bambara. Mali. Wood, height 23$^{1}/_{4}$". Collection Eliot Elisofon, New York

Chi wara dance headdress. Bambara. Mali. Wood, height 17¾″. Collection Pierre Vérité, Paris

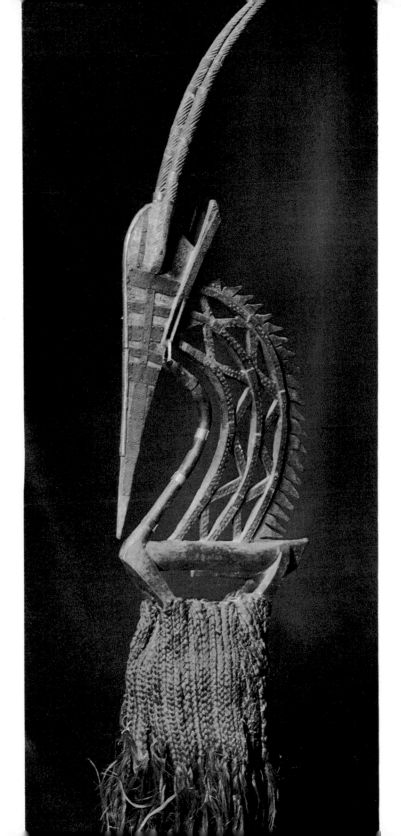

As can be seen here, there are a number of different substyles of these Chi wara headdresses—naturalistic, abstract, vertical, horizontal, doe and fawn motif, and so on. This mask, for instance, is one of the Segu substyle which suggests the roan antelope by a highly decorative patterned mane.

The headdresses of the horizontal type, with their long sweeping horns parallel to their backs, often seem to have an irresistibly personal appeal—the first with its ingratiating smile and curly tail; the other, perhaps a shade supercilious, certainly less forthcoming.

Chi wara dance headdress. Bambara. Mali. Wood,
length 22⁷/₈″. Collection Maurice Nicaud, Paris

◄ Chi wara dance headdress. Bambara. Mali. Wood,
length 20¹/₂″. Collection Pierre Vérité, Paris

The same contrasting qualities of formalism and naturalism are apparent in these two headdresses. The first is a fine abstract of the doe and fawn motif with a pedestal in the place of a body.

Chi wara dance headdress. Bambara. Mali. Wood, height 23^1/$_4$". Formerly Collection Rubinstein, Paris

Chi wara headdress. Bambara. Mali. Wood, height
45¼″. Collection Pierre Vérité, Paris

This carving is as warmly expressive of the
doe and fawn motif as could be imagined.

Dance mask. Mossi. Upper Volta. Wood, height 41³/₈″. Musée Royal de l'Afrique Centrale, Tervueren, Belgium

HEADDRESSES OF VARIOUS KINDS

These tall masks of the Mossi and Bobo must be very difficult to balance, for although they are made of light wood, they are of a great height. They are worn by groups of youths dancing together after the sowing of crops, funeral rituals, or at other times when evil-intentioned spirits might be about. They are also worn by members of the Wango society of the Bobo at a festival for the ripening of certain fruits in the bush. This is an interesting legacy from the days when fruit gathering was important for the subsistence of the tribe.

The face of the mask is highly abstract, and both it and the planklike superstructure are decorated with geometric pattern.

Some masks have a naturalistic figure attached to the top of the plank.

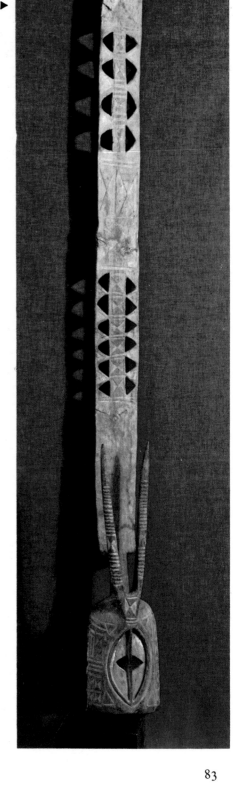

Dance mask. Mossi. Upper
Volta. Wood, height 61″.
Collection Pierre Vérité,
Paris

◀ Dance mask of Do the guar-
dian spirit. Bobo. Upper
Volta. Wood, height 73¹/₄″.
The Museum of Primitive
Art, New York

Two more tall headdresses, but of greater width. It should be noted that all these large, flat headdresses come from the savanna country where the wood is soft and of a light weight.

The rare Senufo headdress is a very fine piece; the three bird finials at the top are symbolic emblems to be found on many Senufo works.

The large "Lorraine Cross" at the top of the Dogon masks is also believed to be symbolic of a bird in flight.

Dance headdress. Dogon. Mali. Wood with fibers, Musée de l'Homme, Paris

Dance headdress mask of the Epa cult. Yoruba. Nigeria. Wood, height 39³/₈″. The British Museum, London

Moving southward into the tropical forest areas of the Guinea Coast and Congo, where timber is hard and heavy, we are at once struck by the very different type of mask which this diversity in material may have caused. It is not simply a question of weight or height. The great Epa masks of the Yoruba may be up to sixty inches in height and weigh eighty pounds or more, but the young men still perform twisting, leaping dances in them. It is rather that the slow cutting-away of the form with adz, gauge, and knife leads to a different kind of approach—more thoughtful, perhaps more planned—resulting in works which often have

Dance headdress mask of the Epa cult. Yoruba. Nigeria. Wood, height 54^3/$_4$". Collection Vincent Price, Beverly Hills, California

an architectural quality of planned proportion or a profusion of detail only to be found in sculpture which may be expected to last for many years, and so be worth the time spent in carving it.

These two Epa mask headdresses illustrate such qualities very clearly. The first, a beautiful old piece, is impressive in its sculptural quality and dignity.

The second is equally impressive in its own way because of its skillful carving, from the solid block, of tier upon tier of small figures surrounding Jagunjagun the warrior.

Headdress for the Ogbom play. Ibo. Nigeria. Wood,
height 33⁷/₈″. Nigerian Museum

The eastern Ibo and the neighboring Ibibio danced a play,
Ogbom, in honor of the earth deity. This no longer takes
place but some of the very fine headdresses are still in existence. This one is particularly impressive in the action of the
dance, for the undercut and pierced upper part of the nose
lets through the light and gives the appearance of a flashing
eye.

The Kuyu of the Congo (Brazzaville), like certain other
Congolese tribes, sometimes seem more interested in surface
pattern than in sculptural form, but this particular piece
gives good value to both.

Otobo water spirit mask. Ibo. Nigeria. Wood, length
26³/₄". The Liverpool Museum

Simo society mask. Baga. Guinea. Wood, length
52³/₄". Collection Nelson Rockefeller, New York.

Very exciting are the large horizontal masks worn slanting on the top of the head by tribes of the coastal and lagoon areas from Guinea to Calabar. For the Ibo and other tribes of the Niger delta and the Ijo of Calabar, these masks are basically box-shaped with abstract features—human, animal, and bird—forming a very fine three-dimensional pattern.

Of those shown here, the Ibo is the most completely abstract. The Baga head is treated differently but combines crocodile teeth and antelope horns with the human face, which is surmounted by a chameleon.

The Ijo mask, which is the finest of the set, is rectangular with strongly formalized human features treated in a cubist fashion.

These masks all represent water spirits; the first and third are strongly suggestive of the hippopotamus.

Otobo water spirit mask. Ijo of Calabar. Nigeria. Wood. The British Museum, London

FIGURE SCULPTURE

CHARACTERISTICS OF TRIBAL FIGURE SCULPTURE

It is not through specific ceremonies alone that the united efforts of both the living and the dead are harnessed to ensure the welfare of the community. It is an affair of daily concern to all. For this reason, carved figures are kept in huts and household shrines and encouraged, through the offering of libations and gifts of food, to participate in family life. We speak of these as ancestor figures when they are set up to receive the spirits of the departed thus incorporating them into the living tribe, or cult figures when they seem to be connected with the activities of definite cults or societies. The first three carvings shown here, however, are used for other purposes.

◀ Fertility doll (Akua'ba), carried by young women. Ashanti. Ghana. Wood, height 14⅝". Collection Arnold Newman, New York

Initiation amulet. Bahungana. Congo. Ivory, ▶ height 4⅜". Musée Royal de l'Afrique Centrale, Tervueren, Belgium

The four figures on these pages illustrate most clearly the Africans' gift for extreme simplification. The first two are almost two-dimensional. Note how the treatment of arms and legs has reduced the body of the Bahungana figure to a diamond surrounded by four triangles.

The second pair consider the figure three-dimensionally. One simplifies it to a zigzag; the other produces a restless complex of cubistic shapes.

Emblem of rank for members of
the Bwami sects. Balega. Congo.
Wood, height 6¹/₄″. Musée
Royal de l'Afrique Centrale,
Tervueren, Belgium

Figure. Ibo. Nigeria. Wood, ▶
height 6³/₄″. The British Museum, London. Talbot Collection

The figure carving of the Bambara is not so abstract as the work shown on the previous pages, but it is reduced to a severely stylized formula, completely static and conveying no sense of movement or emotion.

Of the two pieces shown here, the seated figure is the more naturalistic, yet the carver has obviously felt a need to shorten the arms and enlarge the hands in order to balance the upper part of the figure against the solid mass of buttocks, legs, and stool below.

Ancestor figure. Bambara. Mali. Wood, height 23⅝". The British Museum, London. Christy Collection

Ancestor figure. Bambara. Mali. Wood, height 22^7/$_8$".
Collection Pierre Vérité, Paris

This standing figure shows clearly the common characteristics of Bambara figure sculpture. The neck and trunk are cylindrical, with the trunk fitting into the buttocks as into a socket. The deltoid and pectoralis muscles are treated as one semicircular, flattened area, with the large, conical breasts pointing forward. The arms hang slightly away from the body, palms upward. The knees are bent in both standing and sitting positions; the legs are often shortened and casually carved. These figures may be decorated with pattern.

Many tribes cover their figure carvings with pattern, probably in imitation of their tribal body scarification. This Kuyu figure shows little sense of form; it is merely a convenient support for a mass of pattern.

The Babembe figure, on the other hand, has very interesting formal qualities. It is finely carved and squarely set, with the pattern emphasizing the long, cylindrical trunk.

◀ Serpent cult figure. Kuyu. Congo (Brazzaville). Wood, height 54³/₄″. Collection Pierre Vérité, Paris

Figure. Babembe. Congo (Brazzaville). ▶ Wood, height 62¹/₄″. Sammlung für Völkerkunde der Universität, Zurich

The Dengese carving follows the same lines as the Babembe figure but achieves an impressive monumental effect, not only because of its greater size but because of its dignity and strength. The large, squarely placed hands are a much more effective base for the rising column of the body than the rather weak legs of the Babembe work; and both the rhythm of the form and the regular surface pattern unify the whole.

In the fine old Bena Lulua carving the surface pattern is secondary to the formal qualities of the work.

Figure. Bena Lulua. Congo. Wood, height $26^3/_8$". Musée Royal de l'Afrique Centrale, Tervueren, Belgium

Royal commemorative statue. Dengese. Congo. Wood, height $53^1/_2$". Musée Royal de l'Afrique Centrale, Tervueren, Belgium

97

Ancestor memorial, probably made for neighboring Wabembe tribe. Basikasingo. Congo. Wood, height 25^1/$_4$″. Musée Royal de l'Afrique Centrale, Tervueren, Belgium

These three carvings have been placed together not for sculptural or ethnographical reasons but to give some idea of the tremendous variation of style from tribe to tribe.

The first, with its large triangular head, short legs, and absence of coherent bony structure, has a shaggy, unkempt appearance.

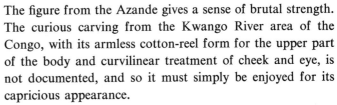

Figure. Azande. Congo. Wood, height
21¹/₄″. The British Museum, London

The figure from the Azande gives a sense of brutal strength.
The curious carving from the Kwango River area of the
Congo, with its armless cotton-reel form for the upper part
of the body and curvilinear treatment of cheek and eye, is
not documented, and so it must simply be enjoyed for its
capricious appearance.

Figure. Kwango River area. Congo.
Wood, height 11″. The British Museum,
London

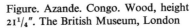

Dogon sculpture is among the most impressive carving of the western Sudan. These pairs of seated figures, so hieratic in appearance and so Egyptian, are made from hard wood and have a natural patina of smoke, oil, and the blood used in sacrificial rites. The sculpture of the Dogon has much in common with that of the neighboring Bambara; noticeably the squared head and long cylindrical neck and trunk, the treatment of the shoulder and breast area, and the apparent lack of interest in the carving of the legs. In both these tribes the carving is done by the smiths.

Ancestor figures. Dogon. Mali. Wood, height 29$\frac{1}{2}$". The Barnes Foundation, Merion, Pennsylvania

◀ Ancestor figures. Dogon. Mali. Wood, height 26$\frac{3}{4}$". Rietberg Museum, Zurich

An older type of carving is to be found hidden in cliffside sanctuaries. Sometimes they have upstretched arms, as in this piece, an attitude possibly indicating prayer to the spirits for rain.

Cult figure. Dogon. Mali. Wood, height 13³/₈″. Musée de l'Homme, Paris

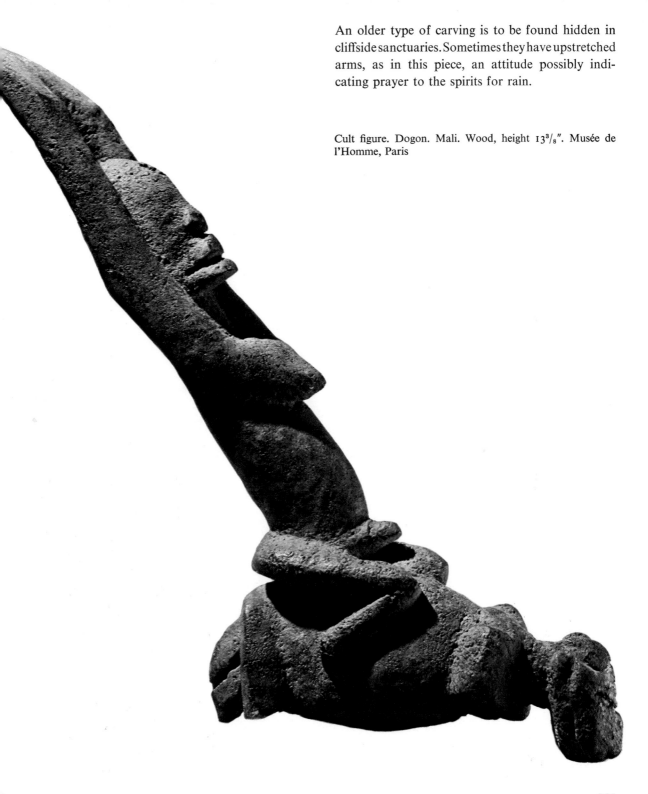

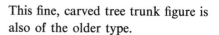
This fine, carved tree trunk figure is also of the older type.

Cult figure. Dogon. Mali. Tree trunk, height 50³/₄″.
Musée de l'Homme, Paris

The young initiates of the Senufo Lo society stamped out in unison the rhythm of their dance with *debles* or rhythm-pounders. These were tall female figures carved from a tree trunk, which the dancers held by the upper arms. The figures had a heavy base which was thumped on the ground to mark the measure of the dance.

This beautiful example, one of the finest of our illustrations, has unfortunately lost the lower portion of the limbs and the solid base, but enough is left for us to appreciate the supple modeling of the shoulders, breasts, and torso and the superb mastery of the treatment of the planes of the face. It is carving of great dignity and appreciation of form.

Figure. Baule. Ivory Coast. Wood, height 18¹/₂″. ▶
The Museum of Primitive Art, New York

Ancestor figure. Baule. Ivory Coast. Wood, height ▶ ▶
24³/₈″. Collection Kamer, Cannes

◀ Ancestor figure. Oron clan of the Ibibio. Nigeria.
Wood. Collection Kenneth Murray, Lagos

The word *gravitas* has been used to express the deep sense of reverence inspired and expressed by many African ancestor figures, and those of the Oron clan of the Ibibio seem most worthy of the term. These are a large collection of ancestor figures of comparatively great age, for some may date back to the early nineteenth century. They stand, holding symbols of office, with something of the quiet dignity of the kings on the great doorway of Chartres cathedral, giving a sense of security in a changing world.

The Baule are noted for their appreciation of good sculpture for genuine aesthetic reasons. Their figure carving and many utilitarian objects, such as loom pulleys, are carved with care and achieve a finish which few African tribes aim to produce. This often results in a rather cloying superficial sweetness, but the best of their work is very good indeed. The figure of the young girl on the next page is a striking example—the simplicity of pose and the lovely flowing line through the trunk, thighs, and legs are delightful.

This small brass casting (it is only about four inches high) has much of the same feeling about it as the carving of the Baule girl on the previous page. But it has more, for the young boy blowing his horn is imbued with tremendous vitality. Ashanti gold weights have long been popular *objets d'art* but few have achieved such mastery of form as this wonderfully fresh and sensitive work.

Weight for gold dust. Ashanti. Ghana. Brass, height 3⅞". The Museum of Primitive Art, New York. Leff Collection

Figure. Probably Temne, ▶
Sierra Leone. Wood, height
39³/₈″. The British Museum,
London

◀ Figure. Temne, Sierra Leone. Wood, height 22⁷/₈″. The
University Museum, Phila-
delphia

The Temne carve figures in some ways like the Minsereh figures of the neighboring Mende. But, whereas the
work of the Mende is rigidly vertical and static, these two Temne carvings bring a fresh vitality to a conventional form, as enlivening in its way as the contribution made by the carver of the hornblower on the
previous page. The svelte lines of these figures give lightness and charm to what could so easily have been
mere ponderous sculptures.

Figure. Senufo. Ivory Coast. Wood, height 39³/₈″.
Collection Pierre Vérité, Paris

A superficial study of African sculpture
might almost suggest that each tribe has
its own clearly recognizable type of mask
or figure carving, constant throughout its
territory and obviously differing from the
work of the tribes which surround it. Nothing could be further from the truth. Tribal
art is influenced by history—by the con-
tacts made during migrations or conquests.
Boundaries do not completely limit contact
between man and man, between carver and
carver. Tribal lands may stretch over a
wide area; the art of the northern branch
of a tribe may conform closely to the work
of its northern neighbors while the art of
the southern members will, in turn, be influenced by the entirely different art of their
neighboring tribe.

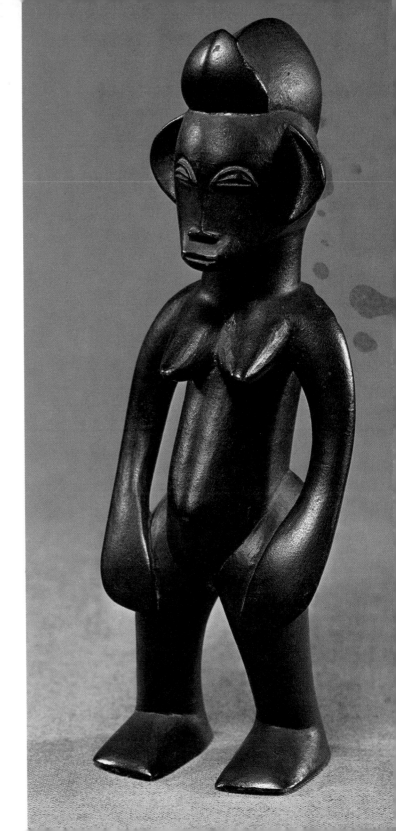

Figure. Senufo. Ivory Coast. Wood, height 7¹/₂″.
National Museum, Copenhagen

The pair of figures shown here are admirable examples of this fact. The work of the northern Senufo shows a clear stylistic affinity with that of the Dogon and Bambara, as in this massive, almost brutal, carving on the left.

But in the south, the Senufo are neighbors of the Guro and Baule, with their entirely different conception of sculptural quality. Here in this small figure we notice at once a sense of flowing rhythm and the highly polished finish of the work.

Yet certain Senufo characteristics are common to both pieces. They can be summed up as a tendency to emphasize angular forward-projecting forms—the chin, the breasts, the navel, the forearms, and the hands. This forward thrust is more emphatic in the smaller carving, and when these or similar figures are seen clearly in profile, it is quickly recognizable by this outstanding characteristic of Senufo work.

Ancestor figure. Bambole. Congo. Wood, height 47¹/₄″. The British Museum, London

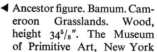

Ancestor figure. Bamum. Cameroon Grasslands. Wood, height 34⁵/₈″. The Museum of Primitive Art, New York

In spite of the grotesque expression of the face, this simple carving of a shackled woman is very moving. The large head, bent slightly forward, together with the slackly hanging arms gives a sense of helpless resignation.

Curiously enough, very much the same emotion is conveyed by the far more subtle Bambole carving. In this piece, the effect is chiefly produced by the curving, hanging legs which can obviously support no weight. Both the beautifully carved head and the whole pose of the hanging figure are sensitively conceived.

Ancestor figure. Bajokwe. Congo. Wood, height 13". Museum für Völkerkunde, Berlin

When we consider the serenely beautiful female masks created by Bajokwe craftsmen, we feel amazed by the uncompromising ugliness of this carving. But the whole strength of Bajokwe art lies in its extreme expressionism. There is no toning down of the portrayal of the human form or of whatever aspect of it they wish to express.

Ancestor figure. Baluba. Congo. Wood, height
35$^3/_8$". Musée Royal de l'Afrique Centrale, Tervueren, Belgium

This large carving is one of the most sensitive sculptures of the Baluba. The quiet,
submissive attitude and the gently modeled
form give the figure great grace. Many
Baluba works have this rather charming
quality of serenity and poise.

Horseman. Bambara. Mali. Wood with fiber, height 32¼″. Collection Pierre Vérité, Paris

HORSEMEN

Disease and lack of suitable pasture make it impossible in many parts of tropical Africa for horses to survive, but where they can be kept, they appear with their riders in sculpture. In the work of the less sophisticated tribes, the animals are sometimes shapeless unrecognizable beasts with no bony structure; in other places, a mythical composite animal is built up, basically horse but with leopard, elephant, or similar additions. Here we show only a few of the more recognizable mounts.

The most naturalistic of them all is from the Bambara. It is a sensitively conceived but straightforward carving of a rider jogging along on his horse. True, he is rather large for his steed, but this signifies that man is more important than beast. Also, if horse and rider were made in a consistent scale, the result would not be so aesthetically satisfactory. This the African carver knows instinctively.

Horseman carrying ritual staffs. Ogboni society for cult of the earth spirits. Yoruba. Nigeria. Ivory, height 14⅝". The British Museum, London

▼

The conventional variation in scale between horse and rider becomes more apparent here. In the Benin bronze it is not remarkable; the two together merely form a comfortable, compact shape.

In the ivory carving the difference in size is enormous, owing to the shape of the tusk from which the work has been carved. The result is, however, quite acceptable and very attractive.

This is a beautifully compact little carving which the sculptor has worked out in a rather extraordinary way. In order to compress the human figure and bring its huge head lower to achieve the solidity of form he needed (or possibly, more prosaically, to fit it all into his chosen piece of wood), the carver has cut out the lower half of the man's body. But the whole effect is convincing, and as before, we are content to abandon naturalism for aesthetic necessity.

Horseman. Yoruba. Nigeria. Wood.
The British Museum, London

Horseman as a caryatid support for divination bowl. Yoruba. Nigeria. Wood, height 9$^1/_2$". Museum für Völkerkunde, Berlin

This short-legged horse and its rider are the support of a wooden bowl used to hold nuts for the divination ceremonies of the Ifa cult. These caryatid figures are of many kinds, and the subject chosen by the sculptor is of no particular significance. In this carving, the height of the horse has been as greatly compressed as that of the man.

No documentation is available for the delightfully comic carving on the opposite page. From stylistic evidence it would appear to come from Abeokuta.

◀ Ejiri or guardian spirit used to control the life force for its owner's ends. Ijo. Nigeria. Wood, height 25⅝". The Museum of Primitive Art, New York

Figure. Bayaka. Congo. Wood, height 9½". ▶ Musée Royal de l'Afrique Centrale, Tervueren, Belgium

◀ This creature is not a horse at all, but a composite monster incorporating various animal forms—elephant ears, leopard teeth, and so on—giving a total impression of great strength. It is not connected with any ancestor or spirit cult but is a powerful object used to obtain success for its owner.

THE MOTHER AND CHILD MOTIF

The mother and child motif is found among the sculpture of many African tribes. It is pre-Christian in most areas, although on the Guinea coast and in the western Congo it must have been influenced by early Christian missions.

Very different from the grotesque little figures usually associated with the Bayaka is this mother and child. Crude as the sculpture is in some respects, it is one of the very few African carvings of this subject that suggests an emotional active response between mother and child. Another with similar feeling from the neighboring Bambala tribe is illustrated later.

Figure of mother and child. Bena Lulua. Congo. Wood, height 14$\frac{1}{8}$″. Musée Royal de l'Afrique Centrale, Tervueren, Belgium

This Bena Lulua mother is very static and expressionless. She clutches her child as though it were a sack of potatoes. The figure itself shows the tribe's strong appreciation of surface decoration.

Head of a staff, with mother and child motif. Dogon. Mali. Wood, height 22⁷/₈″. The Museum of Primitive Art, New York. Leff Collection

In this Dogon work, we are still further removed from a sense of human relationship. We meet, instead, an extraordinarily attractive abstract design in the round which forms the top of a staff.

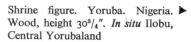

Shrine figure. Yoruba. Nigeria. ▶
Wood, height 30³/₄". *In situ* Ilobu,
Central Yorubaland

Although they come from very different tribal
backgrounds, these two sculptures would seem
to have much in common. Both are statuesque.
The first, by merit of its greater size and stylized
treatment, may be termed monumental. It is
indeed an impressive figure.

The second, freer in its pose, is in sculptural
terms the greater of the two works. It achieves a
splendid rhythm and vitality through the repeat-
ed curves of the thigh, arm, breasts, and chin,
while losing nothing of its calm dignity. There is
no cloying sentimentality in such representations
of human motherhood, but rather an acknowl-
edgment of the mysterious forces of fertility
which lie in the hands of the ancestors and the
gods.

Ancestor figure. Bambara. Mali.
Wood, height 49¹/₄". The Museum
of Primitive Art, New York

Figure with child. Bambala. Congo. Wood, ▶ height 20½″. Ethnografisch Museum, Antwerp

Figure with children. Afo. Nigeria. Wood, height 23⅝″. The Horniman Museum, London

The Afo mother with her several children is an interesting and powerful work. The linear scarifications emphasize the many long, cylindrical shapes and give the whole piece a dry, restless, stringy effect. Everything seems to be shooting off the main axis at an oblique angle and yet to be held together by unseen centripetal forces.

The Bambala mother, on the other hand, seems curiously familiar, as if she might be posing with her child for a conventional photograph. So strong is this impression that only slowly does one notice curious divergencies from the naturalistic, such as the extreme shortening of the legs.

Shango cult figure. Yoruba. Nigeria. Wood, height 16⁷/₈″. Collection René d'Harnon-court, New York

This piece is one of the most beautiful African carvings of the mother and child, with its rhythmic, flowing curves overlying a suggestion of bodily strength—a representation of idealized motherhood. It was collected some twenty years ago in a Shango temple where women are the devotees and servants of the god, who in turn may be expected to ensure their fertility.

Figure with bowl. Bafum. Cameroon Grasslands. Wood, height 37³/₈″. Museum für Völkerkunde, Berlin

Figure with bowl. Bikom. Cameroon Grasslands. Wood, height 29¹/₈″. Museum für Völkerkunde, Berlin. Glanning Collection

FIGURES HOLDING BOWLS

In the Cameroon Grasslands, figures holding bowls such as these are used when offerings are made to the spirits.

We have noted above the vitality, almost amounting to buffoonery, in masks from this area. Here the carvings show the same quality of rugged strength, but pathos is also expressed—their owner is using them to seek help in his necessity.

This is perhaps the most lovely of the dozen sculptures in the "long-faced style" of the village of Buli in Baluba country. The head, with its long straight nose and thin lips, is Hamitic in type, finely proportioned, and of great beauty.

Figure with bowl. Baluba. Congo. Wood,
height 13³/₄″. National Museum, Copenhagen

It is interesting to compare this more
typical Baluba figure with that from
Buli, on the opposite page. The spare,
angular figure with its more realistic
proportion is in great contrast; yet it,
too, is a very fine carving.

Ifa is a most important Yoruba cult, concerned with a system of divination based on the number sixteen and its multiples. Most Ifa figures carry bowls to contain the nuts used in the ceremonies. The compact little ivory figure has great dignity.

Ifa cult figure. Yoruba. Nigeria. Wood, height 13³/₈". National Museum, Copenhagen

Ifa cult figure. Yoruba. Nigeria. Ivory, height 7¹/₂". ▶
The British Museum, London

Fitness for purpose is an important rule for any craftsman, and a stool must not only be capable of taking weight but must also look as though it can do so. The two great Atlaslike figures, which, standing back to back, support the stool, are splendidly designed for this purpose. With great economy of line and form, the strong trunk and limbs are set foursquare and immovable.

Caryatid stool. Ashanti. Ghana. Wood, height 28⅜″. The British Museum, London

▲

Caryatid stool. Basonge-Baluba. Congo. Wood, height 23¼″. Musée Royal de l'Afrique Centrale, Tervueren, Belgium

suring hands, strong grooved neck, and slightly bent head suggest great concentration. On all other counts, too, this is a beautiful and sensitive work.

Caryatid bowl. Basonge. Congo. Wood, height 20⅛″. The British Museum, London. Plass Collection

▼

The fantastic figure on the left appears completely unconcerned about her function as a weight bearer. Such a well-built, cheerful soul should be able to take the strain!

The carving on the right expresses its adequacy for the purpose through the tension of the figure. The slightly bent knees, tensely held arms, reas-

Caryatid stool. Afo. Nigeria. Wood, height
$22^1/_2''$. Museum für Völkerkunde, Berlin

The Afo carving is unconvincing as a stool. It looks neither secure nor comfortable, but, as a piece of sculpture, it is a most vigorous and striking work. The lines of the legs and upstretched arms form one rhythm and the long pendulous breasts and similarly shaped thighs form another in a different plane. The whole is firmly held together by the large heads and the horizontal top of the stool.

Caryatid stool. Baluba. Congo. Wood, height 21¹/₄″.
The British Museum, London

This beautiful stool is one of the famous works from the little village of Buli in Baluba country. Here the carver has tackled his subject in his own inimitable way; the enormous head and hands, so sensitively carved that they never appear overpowering, create a rhythm and balance in the figure as a whole which is most satisfying.

Finally a Dahomey figure supporting a large and heavy bowl is placed here to be seen in relation to the Buli stool on the facing page. It is a very small work, only seven and one-half inches high, yet it has a surprisingly monumental quality. Its keynote, in contrast to the calm of the Buli stool, is tension. The rounded form shows no sign of muscle in action but every limb is keyed up to the task of balancing that heavy bowl. Head and arms well back, breasts tensed upward, and toes tucked in under the buttocks give a feeling of only minute-to-minute poise in the effort to keep the bowl from tilting forward.

Headrest. Bakuba. Congo. Wood, height $7^1/_8''$. Musée
Royal de l'Afrique Centrale, Tervueren, Belgium

The functional requirements of a headrest are very difficult for a nonuser to judge. The exact height is presumably a matter of personal preference, as is the correct curve of the top. Of the two shown on these pages, the Bakuba is far the less sophisticated, but it is an impressive piece of work in an unpolished peasant-art kind of way.

This headrest is more pretentious. The two-headed support is very well designed and balanced for its purpose and the top and base are fittingly decorated. It looks useful and practical, but at the same time has rhythm in its form.

Headrest. Basuka. Congo. Wood, height $5\frac{1}{8}''$. Musée Royal de l'Afrique Centrale, Tervueren, Belgium

The double-figured headrests illustrated on these two pages are in an entirely different category from the pair previously shown. The headrest on the left is Baluba, the one on the right comes from the more narrowly defined area of the village of Buli in Baluba country. They are both works of very high aesthetic quality, and the choice between them is a matter of personal preference.

The one on the left is solid and concentrated. As so often happens, it brings a conviction that the African standard of proportion is much better aesthetically than that of real life, for the whole satisfaction of this piece lies in the rhythm and balance achieved by the unrealistic proportion of its masses.

In this carving, the rhythm of the work is felt as much in the spaces left between the parts as in the masses themselves. The greatly enlarged heads, Hamitic in type, are carved with very great sensitivity, while the strong flat hands, so typically a part of the Buli idiom, are convincingly right.

These Buli works, of which only a dozen have been found, consist of caryatids, figures holding bowls, and standing figures. They may be the work of one or several sculptors. Their aesthetic appeal is as universal and of much the same kind as that of the best European early Gothic sculpture.

◀ Headrest. Baluba. Congo. Wood, height 7¹/₈″. Collection Charles Ratton, Paris

Headrest. Baluba. Congo. Ivory, height 6¹/₄″. Collection Charles Ratton, Paris
▼

Finally in this group come two more Baluba headrests, pieces of contrasting moods.

The first portrays a bhang (Indian hemp) smoker with his calabash water pipe. It is all sharp angles, tensions, and restless movement. Several other works in the same style have been collected, and they have become known as the "cascade style" from the curious setting of the hair.

The ivory headrest, on the other hand, is quietly static. The vertical lines of the body are neatly contained by the horizontal top and base. It is symmetrical and naturalistic, with a directness and simplicity which is very restful.

FETISH FIGURES

A fetish is literally a parcel of ingredients kept in a horn or bundle as the locus of a destructive power which will operate at its owner's behest provided he maintains and appeases it with regular offerings.

Fetish figures therefore are technically supports for fetish material which is hung around them in bundles or horns or alternatively concealed in an orifice in the stomach or anus. The ownership of such material gives a man tremendous power over others, and fear of a reputedly powerful fetish will cause a guilty person to take almost any step to protect himself from it. The medicine man or witch doctor from whom such fetishes can be obtained stands in a unique position in the community.

There also appear to be figures containing no fetish material but which are greatly feared and unto which propitiatory sacrifices are made.

Diviner consulting a gourd of oil. Mwanza. Tanzania

Fetish figure. Basonge. Congo. Wood with feathers, fibers, beads, etc., height 37³/₄″. Musée Royal de l'Afrique Centrale, Tervueren, Belgium

The definition of a fetish figure as one carrying fetish material, such as ground-up bone, teeth, claws, leaves, hair, blood, bile, and excreta, differentiates it from an ancestor or cult figure believed to house a departed spirit.

In these three most impressive and powerful fetishes, the first two show orifices in the stomach to hold the "medicine," while the third is carrying it packed in the horns slung over its arm. The power of the second is greatly increased by the big iron bells which it carries in addition to the hornful of "medicine" on its head.

◀ Fetish figure. Basonge. Congo. Wood, beads, metal, horn, and iron bells, height 40¹/₂″. The British Museum, London

Hermaphrodite fetish figure. Basuku. Congo. Wood with horns, ▶ height 23¹/₄″. Musée Royal de l'Afrique Centrale, Tervueren, Belgium

Fetish figure. Lower Congo. Wood with fiber, etc., ▶
height 29¹/₈″. Musée Royal de l'Afrique Centrale, Tervueren, Belgium

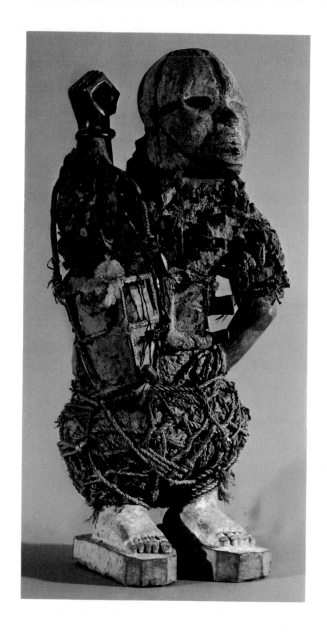

Fetish figure. Bahungana. Congo. Wood, height 15³/₄″. Museum für Völkerkunde, Berlin

144

Nail fetish figure. Bakongo. Congo. Wood with iron nails and wedges. The British Museum, London

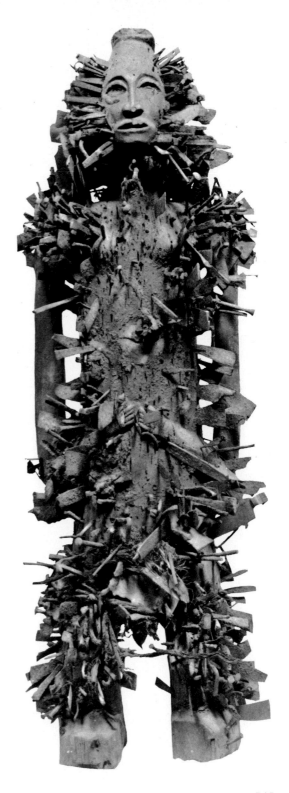

The Lower Congo figure on the left is encrusted with reddish fetish material with which it has been anointed. It also has a number of nails or wedges driven into it. The upraised hand originally held a spear.

The curious little Bahungana figure would have had "medicine" in the bag slung from its waist and probably in the pot carved on the top of its head. The many miniature figures hanging round it are all part of its equipment.

Nail fetishes are peculiar to the Bakongo. They are used, as directed by the witch doctor, for either aggressive or protective purposes. The client drives a nail into the wooden body each time he makes use of the magical power which it contains.

Fetish figure with mirror. Bakongo. Congo. Wood, height 10¼″. The Allen Memorial Art Museum, Oberlin, Ohio

The fetish on this page has a large cavity in its abdomen to contain the "medicine." This is covered by a piece of mirror, in itself a powerful force.

The two fetishes opposite are of very different sizes, the one from the Cameroons being only about eight inches high and the Bapende about forty-nine inches. Yet they both have an intensely spooky appearance. This could have been fortuitous in the first case, but the large Bapende work has surely been created by a sculptor who knew what he was about and who intended to convey a powerful sense of the supernatural. It is one of the most expressive works of African sculpture.

Fetish figure. Bapende. Congo. Wood, height 48⁷/₈″. ▶
Musée de la Vie Indigène, Leopoldville

Fetish figure. Cameroons. Stick with modeled wax
head and bust, height 7⁷/₈″.

Six-headed fetish. Baluba. Congo. Wood, copper ▶
strips, animal hide, and raffia cloth, height 18⁷/₈″.
The British Museum, London

Figure. Southern Kasai. Congo. Wood, height
24³/₈″. Musée Royal de l'Afrique Centrale, Tervueren, Belgium

Some figures, although not fetishes in the
strict sense of containing fetish material,
are looked upon as having strong malevolent powers. For instance, members of
the Lilwa society of the Bambole in the
Congo executed criminals and retained
their power in figures which were then
believed to watch over the community.
(As far as the community was concerned
they might then be considered benevolent!)

The Kasai effigy, documented as "a
very dangerous and destructive figure," may
have been something of this kind but
nothing concrete is recorded of it.

The beautiful six-headed Baluba fetish
shown opposite would appear to be of an
entirely different character. Each head is
delicately modeled with all the charm nor-
mally found in Baluba carving. One would
like to feel it was a fetish dedicated to
protective purposes alone.

Fetish figure. Baluba. Congo. Wood with animal hide, snail shells, and calabash, height 15″. Collection Tristan Tzara, Paris

Finally this Baluba fetish shows the same beautiful modeling as the last. It is certain that fetishes are used to control the forces of nature—to ensure fertility, protection, the cure of disease, and so on—and not merely to inflict harm on the owner's enemies. Yet we should guard against reading our own interpretation into the aspect of such sculpture as this, remembering that the power of the piece is supposed to lie in the "medicine" which it contains, and which will be released, subject to the performance of the right rituals, simply according to the good or evil desires of the owner.

Reliquary figure. Bakota. Gabon. Wood, height 22⁷/₈″. The University Museum, Philadelphia

RELIQUARIES

Reliquary figures carved to stand above basket or barkcloth receptacles containing the bones of ancestors are common among the Bakota and Fang of Gabon. Some are also found among the Ambete to the south of the Bakota, but are rarely found among tribes in other areas.

The figures do not represent the ancestors themselves; rather, they are the guardians of the bones, placed there to ward off evil which might desecrate the ancestral remains.

Reliquary figure. Bakota. Gabon. Wood bound ▶ with strips of metal. Musée de l'Homme, Paris

Reliquary figure. Bakota. Gabon. Brass-plated wood, height 16½". Collection O. le Corneur, Paris
▼

Figures bound with metal strips are believed to be older than those which are plated with sheets of brass or copper. The lozenge-shaped body in the top illustration is a residual shape from the similar form of the three-dimensional carving shown first in this series, and is possibly a representation of arms held akimbo.

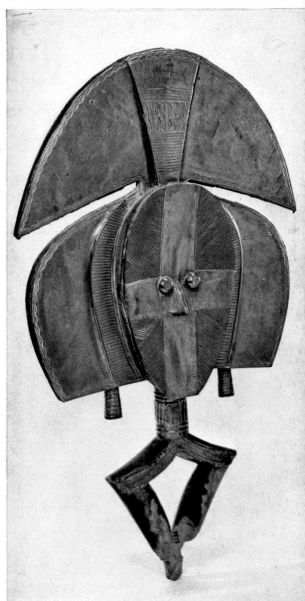

◀ Reliquary figure with bag containing relics. Bakota. Gabon. Wood ornamented with metal strips, feathers, fiber, and hide, height 22½″. Musée de l'Homme, Paris

Reliquary figure. Bakota. Gabon. Wood with copper and brass sheeting, height 31½″. Ethnological Collection, Zurich

▼

Here we see the total effect of the reliquary surmounted by its guardian figure.

The figure on the right is made interesting by the combination of copper and brass sheeting further decorated with engraved lines.

Reliquary head. Fang. Gabon. Wood, height 18¹/₂″. The Museum of Primitive Art, New York

Reliquary figure. Fang. Gabon. Wood, height 25⁵/₈″. The Museum of Primitive Art, New York

In the figure carving of the Fang, a richly sensual delight in the softly flowing curves of the human body is paramount. This is emphasized by the highly polished finish of their sculpture. Yet there is nothing superficial in the sculptor's perception. The body and limbs are well articulated and the figures show a real grasp of the underlying structure. These qualities can be felt in all their reliquary figures illustrated here.

The carvings of separate reliquary heads have a quality which is quite different from that of the heads carved as part of the figure sculptures. These separate heads have the same delight in rhythmic form but the work is refined and there is not an ounce of superficial flesh left anywhere. The carving is reduced almost to abstraction, and the result is beautiful and deeply moving.

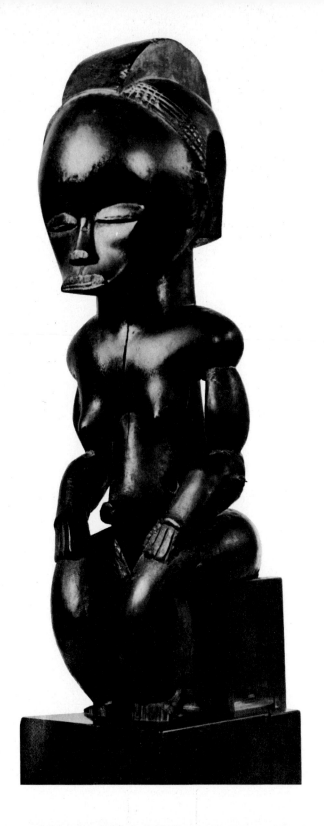

Reliquary figure. Fang. Gabon. Wood,
height 17³/₈″. Formerly Collection Epstein.

Reliquary figure. Fang. Gabon. Wood.
The British Museum, London. Plass Collection

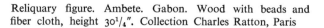

Reliquary figure. Ambete. Gabon. Wood with beads and fiber cloth, height 30¼". Collection Charles Ratton, Paris

The large reliquary figures of this tribe are in great contrast to the sophisticated refinement of the Fang carving. They are interesting in that no bag holding ancestral bones is attached; instead, the bones are packed into a cavity in the body, which opens at the back.

THE SCULPTURE OF SOME ANCIENT AFRICAN KINGDOMS

So far we have considered African sculpture as it was created, to gain spiritual help for the community or the individual in the hazards of daily life, and associated the purpose for which the carving was made with our appreciation of its aesthetic value.

But there are other considerations to be taken into account. We should wish to know something of the history of these works and whether any attempt can be made to date them. In a country where tropical conditions and insect life can destroy all but the toughest material overnight and where such durable materials are rare—a country, moreover, where men took no thought of the aesthetic value of their possessions and made little effort to preserve them—it is difficult to make reliable statements as to the age of most of the work. Little wood carving can have survived for more than a century or two. But stone, terra cotta, and metal last much longer, and radiocarbon methods have dated the deposits containing the Nok terra cottas, the earliest African sculpture yet discovered, back to between 500 B.C. and A.D. 200. The Nok culture, which takes its name from the village where the first pieces were found, stretched over a wide area in the southern part of Nigeria's Northern Provinces. The finds consist of fragments of large terra-cotta figures of which the heads are in the best state of preservation.

Then comes a gap of a thousand years in our knowledge, and the next great culture of which we have evidence is that of Ife, which has always held a position of special veneration in south Yorubaland. William Fagg has suggested a connection between their work and that of Nok in the distant past. Be that as it may, both style and tradition claim it as the forerunner of Benin art, at least since the early fifteenth century, when a master bronze founder was sent by the Oni of Ife to the Oba of Benin to instruct his people in the art of metal casting. Bronze casting from the Lower Niger and from Dahomey and Ghana are also illustrated in this section; as well as portrait statues in wood from the Congo kingdom of the Bakuba.

Stone is comparatively rarely used in Africa, but interesting monoliths and figure carvings have been found in sacred spots in the forests of Nigeria. These are represented here by two carvings from the Ekoi of the Upper Cross River in the southeast of that country. Old soapstone carvings from Liberia and the Lower Congo are also shown. Finally come the great stone walls of Zimbabwe in Rhodesia, always considered to be one of the mysteries of the continent.

Elephant head. Nok. Northern Nigeria. Terra cotta. The British Museum, London

◀ Head. Nok. Northern Nigeria. Terra cotta, height 9″. Nigerian National Museums

Head. Nok. Northern Nigeria. Terra cotta, height 4³/₄″. Nigerian National Museums
▼

NOK

These three heads, fragments from full-figure sculptures, show the diversity and yet unity of the Nok style. The almost constant feature is the pierced pupil of the eye; the orifices of the nose and ear are also often pierced and the borders of the area of the eye are clearly marked by either a triangular or an elliptical form.

The reduction of the features in these heads to a well co-ordinated assemblage of simple shapes is impressive.

Head. Ancient Ife. Nigeria. Terra cotta. The British Museum, London

Head. Ancient Ife. Nigeria. Terra cotta. The Oni of Ife

IFE

The sculpture of Ife and more particularly the terra-cotta and bronze heads present a most intriguing problem to the archaeologist. The first heads to be found were dug up in 1910. Since then, a great deal of excavation has gone on in and around the palace grounds at Ife but no incontrovertible clue has yet been found to date the sculpture.

Briefly, the heads are quite unlike any other genuine African work, being fully naturalistic and visualized intellectually rather than emotionally. They are studied, scientifically proportioned, and very impressive, but the conception is more like that of the Greeks than anything else. Yet of foreign influence there is no trace. Most cultures can be studied from their beginning to their zenith; Ife sculpture suddenly appears, full grown. Nothing leads up to it, so nothing can lead us back to its origins. Under the circumstances, it is tempting to postulate the development of an intermediate culture—still buried and undiscovered—which served as a bridge between the known work of the Nok and the Ife carvings a thousand years later.

Head. Ancient Ife. Nigeria. Bronze, height 12⅝″. Nigerian National Museums

These two bronzes again show the measured realism of the work of ancient Ife. In the first head the subtle modeling of the bony structure felt beneath the flesh is most sophisticated, while the royal half-statue of the Oni in full regalia is maturely conceived and worked out with tremendous attention to detail.

Half-statue of an Oni of Ife. Ancient Ife. Nigeria. Bronze, height 14⅝". Nigerian National Museums

Head of a Queen Mother. Early period. Benin. Nigeria. Bronze, height 16$\frac{1}{8}$". The British Museum, London

BENIN

From both style and tradition it may safely be said that Benin art was, in the earliest stage in which we find it, strongly influenced by that of Ife. It shows the same naturalism and the same appreciation of the subtle fullness of flesh over bony structure that is such an essential quality of Ife work. Our example of this early period is the beautiful head of a Queen Mother, a work of idealized naturalism. It probably dates from the early sixteenth century.

As time passed this strong naturalism, most likely derived from the Ife and foreign to most African art, was replaced by a more conceptual vision. The piece from the second or middle period, probably seventeenth century, is hardly a fair example to use, for unlike the other two, it may have been connected with a spirit cult and not be a royal memorial. In it the artist has given full rein to symbols of magical power—ibises, snakes, frogs, and so on. It is a very lively, powerful piece compared with the placid beauty of the Queen Mother.

Finally in the early nineteenth century the work deterioriated. It was neither intellectually nor emotionally conceived, and objects such as the winged head shown opposite, which stood on the royal altar, became mere solid, useful supports for the carved tusks. The sequence of these various styles has been worked out by William Fagg by correlation with the bronze wall plaques, which are more easy to date positively.

Ritual head, probably for a spirit cult. Middle period. ▶
Benin. Nigeria. Bronze, height $10^5/_8''$. The British
Museum, London

◀ Memorial head. Late period. Benin. Nigeria.
Bronze. Museum für Völkerkunde, Vienna

167

◄ Pectoral mask. Benin. Nigeria. Ivory, height 9⁷/₈″.
The Museum of Primitive Art, New York

This very fine ivory is a small regalia mask worn, hung at the waist, by the Oba at certain ceremonies. From its style, it is a work of the early period, but could not have been made before the beginning of the sixteenth century because the heads which form the decoration on the head and neck represent the Portuguese.

LOWER NIGER

Seated figure. Tada. Northern Nigeria. Bronze, height 20¹/₂″. *In situ* Tada

Bronzes were also cast at other centers, and for some years it has been realized that a very exciting style of bronze casting stemmed from some source in the Lower Niger. Some pieces have been found as far afield as Jebba and Tada on the Upper Niger, but tradition has it that they were brought there from Idah on the Lower Niger by Tsoede, a culture hero. The magnificent seated figure from Tada clearly derives from the Ife traditional style and is in a class by itself.

The rest, of which our Jebba head and the Hunter on the following pages are examples, show the special quality which unites them all. They are entirely conceptual in character, alive and vivid, sometimes to the point of violence. The Hunter conveys this emotional response most clearly; the limp, dead antelope, the lively little dog, and the strength of the man himself are magnificently portrayed. Measured proportion is of no importance; the shortness of the legs is even emphasized by the curious genuflecting stance, but this in no way impairs the realism of the piece.

Head of a figure of a bowman. Jebba. Northern ▶
Nigeria. Bronze, height of full figure 37″. Jebba
Gungu Village

Figure of a hunter. Lower Niger. Nigeria.
Bronze, height 14⅝″. The British Museum,
London
▼

Farther to the west, the peoples of both Dahomey and Ghana practiced the art of metal casting, as these illustrations show.

The first, a brass figure over forty inches high, is made of sheets of metal riveted together. It may belong to the cult of Gu, the god of war of the Fon, a notably warlike tribe. The technique is at variance with the usual craftsmanship of the Guinea area, and may have developed from ideas imported from abroad.

Shrine figure. Fon. Dahomey. Brass, height 41″. Collection Charles Ratton, Paris

Mask. Bron. Ghana. Brass, height 7⅞″. The Museum of Primitive Art, New York

Mask. Ashanti. Ghana. Gold, height $7^1/_8''$. The Wallace Collection, London

The two masks are impressive examples of a more traditional type of work; the Bron may be considered aesthetically the greater. Human in feature yet animal in general form, it has a poetic quality which the massive and more straightforward gold mask lacks.

Royal statue. Bakuba. Congo. Wood, height 22″.
The British Museum, London

BAKUBA

The Bakuba claim that traditions of their kingdom go back some fifteen hundred years. A number of royal statues exist, which are said to have been carved during the lifetime of the king portrayed, though this is doubtful in some cases.

This one is of Shamba Bolongongo, always considered to have been the greatest of all the rulers, a leader in social reform and a patron of the arts. He reigned early in the sixteenth century.

Royal statue. Bakuba. Congo. Wood, height 20¹/₈″. Musée Royal de l'Afrique Centrale, Tervueren, Belgium

The king portrayed in this statue is Kata Mbula, the one hundred and ninth in the succession. The statues are all very similar. Each king sits cross-legged, staring before him, and is to be identified by the object which he holds—an anvil, a game board, a pestle and mortar, and so on. The Bakuba are chiefly renowned for their decorative art; they make a great variety of colored and beaded masks, embroidered textiles, boxes, and decorated wooden cups for palm wine.

◀ Monolithic carving, said to be memorial of a priest-king. Ekoi. Cross River, Nigeria. Hard basalt, height above ground 50³/₄″. *In situ*

Head of monolithic carving, said to be memorial of a priest-king. Ekoi. Cross River, Nigeria. Hard basalt, height including beard 14¹/₈″. *In situ*

MONOLITHS FROM THE CROSS RIVER AREA

These sculptures are two of some three hundred carvings to be found grouped in the centers of old villages on the banks of the Middle Cross River. They are said to have been carved by the Ekoi in memory of their ancestors. Oral tradition has it that they are very old, and it is considered that they may date anywhere from A.D. 1600 to 1900.

The monoliths of rock are shaped and smoothed. Some are engraved rather than carved, as is the one on the left; others have only the facial features and the navel worked in high relief, as the head on the right. Both types are very impressive.

Nomoli figure. Mende. Sierra Leone. Soapstone, height 4³/₄″. The Baltimore Museum of Art

Group of figures. Kissi. Guinea. Soapstone, height 15″. Collection Maurice Nicaud, Paris

MENDE AND KISSI

Small soapstone figures known as *nomoli* are found buried in the ground in parts of Sierra Leone and Guinea. They are probably relics of an earlier civilization, but are now used by the Mende and Kissi as rice gods to bring a rich harvest. They usually have disproportionately large heads with bulgy eyes and huge noses and lips. The body carving is less developed and the whole figure is held together as a sculptural mass.

Both these carvings suggest a group of people.

178

Figure of mother and child. Bakongo. Lower Congo.
Soapstone, height 16⅞". The British Museum, London

BAKONGO

This soapstone mother and child from the
Bakongo, which may be several hundred
years old, is stylistically very like the more
modern wood carving of that tribe. Indeed,
it is treated in a way more suited to wood
carving than to stone. Note, for instance, the
piercing and removal of the material beneath
the arms and compare it with the unbroken
compact mass of the Mende figure.

View of part of the interior of the Elliptical Building or Palace, formerly called "the Temple." Zimbabwe

ZIMBABWE

The rediscovery of Zimbabwe in the second half of the nineteenth century aroused tremendous romantic enthusiasm, for it held all the ingredients of an historic thriller. It had, of course, been known long before to both Arabs and Portuguese, and it is probably due to Arab folklore passed on by the later Portuguese discoverers that these vast stone walls were ascribed to Solomon and the Queen of Sheba, colorful characters in both Moslem and Christian tradition.

The description of the great ruins by Mauch, a German geologist, in 1871 was followed by a succession of explorers, some of whom indulged in regrettably destructive digging; but slowly the mysterious settlements— for there were others besides those of Zimbabwe itself in the locality—were studied more scientifically from various angles. Work was done on chronological dating of types of local artifacts found on the site; these were then cross-dated with Chinese, Persian, and Arab importations found in the middens. Building methods employed both in the laying of the stone walls, and in the construction of the pole and *daga* (or earth) huts, the remains of which were found at various levels in the deposits within the walls, were also studied. Of the successive workers on the site, Miss Caton-Thompson, whose *Zimbabwe Culture* is still a classic, was one of the soundest. She suggested the eighth or ninth centuries as the time of the earliest occupation of the site, and the thirteenth century as its peak period, and supported her thesis by evidence from her field work, which could not be lightly brushed aside.

Further researchers, working from both archaeological and anthropological angles and finally from the results of radiocarbon tests, have produced a table suggesting the earliest pottery found on the site to date from about A.D. 330. The first and second types of wall appear to have been built successively between 1450 and 1830, and the third possibly even later.

So provisionally we picture this sacred settlement of Zimbabwe, situated on a hilltop at the head of a valley, watered by rains brought from the Indian Ocean by the southeast winds; a site where not only was the climate good, but where excellent stone for building abounded and rich deposits of gold for trade lay in the surrounding areas. Its earliest settlers may have come down from East Africa in the Rhodesian Iron Age— say during the fourth century A.D. In the late eleventh century they were building wattle-and-daub huts and owned Zebu-type cattle. Both tradition and ethnographical evidence suggest that they built up a confederacy ruled by a dynasty which called itself Monomatapa. These were replaced later by the Rozwi Mambos who built the splendid stone walls.

According to radiocarbon dating, the peak period of these walls of roughly faced and dressed stone laid in regular courses, when most of the Acropolis walls and the famous conical tower were built, may have been as late as 1830. Zimbabwe must have been a wealthy trading center visited by Arabs and Portuguese, but finally it deteriorated and vanished so completely that little clue has so far been found as to its detailed history.

Entrance to the Elliptical Building. Zimbabwe

Drum. Baule. Ivory Coast. Wood, height 90½″.
Musée de l'Homme, Paris

This drum is a splendid example of informal decoration. The carving, in various levels of high and low relief, ranges from fairly naturalistic figures to incised geometrical patterns and holds together in a very well-balanced manner in spite of its seeming inconsistency.

DECORATIVE OR APPLIED ART IN AFRICA

From sculpture—usually regarded as one of the freest and most uncommitted forms of art, but as we have seen in Africa, often deeply involved in religious or hierarchical observances—we turn to applied art.

Here fitness for purpose is an accepted criterion. But an artist in this field must not only understand the purpose to which an object will be put; he must also show sensitivity and understanding of both the material and the tools which he is using.

Carving completely in the round, in high relief or in low relief, has, in each case, a character of its own. Again carved wood, modeled clay, or cast bronze may each be worked in the round or in low or high relief. Added to this, each material has an individuality of its own, and so have each of the different techniques employed. A true craftsman has a genuine understanding of and a sympathy with all these various qualities of form, texture, and working and so he utilizes them with respect. Similarly, the weaving of pattern into the very texture of a screen or textile, the printing of a pattern on the surface of a ready-woven cloth, or the engraving of a design upon a hard surface, all call for appropriate individual treatment at the hands of a sensitive craftsman.

The African is at home with his materials; he has lived surrounded by them from his childhood and he knows how they work. It is our modern civilization, with its welter of synthetic substances and its plethora of machinery, which is in danger of losing the way.

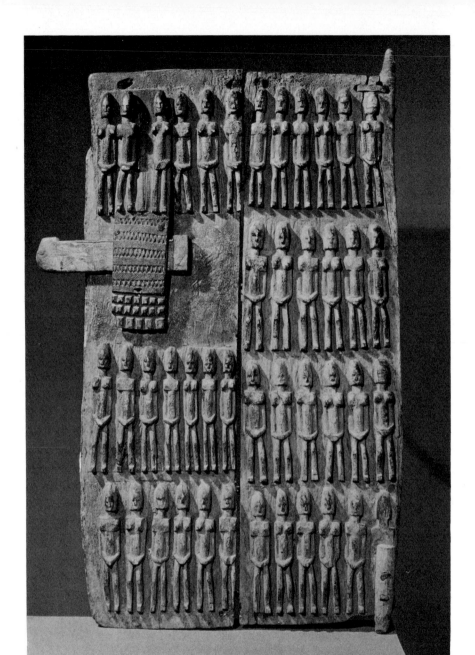

Granary door. Dogon. Mali. Wood. The Museum of Primitive Art, New York

DOORS, PANELS, PLAQUES, SCREENS, AND WALL PAINTINGS

This very fine door panel gets its decorative effect from the regularity of the ranks of female figures.

In this door the carving of the forms is less regimented than in the first work. The grazing animals are in fairly regular formation along the base, but are more loosely constructed, as are the horsemen at the top. Large birds and lizards fill up the unused spaces very satisfactorily.

Granary door. Senufo. Northern Ivory Coast. Wood, height 51⁵/₈″. Collection André Held, Ecublens, Switzerland

◀ Palace door. Yoruba. Nigeria. Wood, height 115³/₈″. The British Museum, London

▲

Palace wall panel. Dahomey. Clay, height 28³/₄″. Palace of Agadja, Dahomey

This palace door is far more sophisticated and technically accomplished than the granary doors shown previously. Scenes of African life are depicted in each panel, riders on horseback and bicycles; women pounding; porters with loads—all the bustle and argument of daily life. Yet the effect of the whole is never lost in the multiplicity of detail.

In interesting contrast is the clay panel from Dahomey. Far bolder and more simple than the hardwood door (as befits its fragile material), this scene of an early missionary arriving from overseas is splendidly designed to fit the square panel.

The bronze plaques of Benin exemplify court art, or "man-regarding art," at its most conventional.

A seventeenth-century Dutch writer said of the Oba's palace in 1668, "Its roof rests on wooden pillars covered from top to bottom with cast copper, engraved with war deeds and battles." Needless to say, these plaques were made by the Oba's special craftsmen and designed to set forth his glory and power. The piece shown below represents the Oba seated with an attendant chief on either side; the little Portuguese figures in the background are said to symbolize status and power.

Plaque. Benin. Nigeria. Bronze, height 20¹/₂″. The British Museum, London

When collected together, such works have a monotonous, mass-produced effect. Nevertheless, there are a number of very fine pieces—some delicate and sensitive in their engraving, others strong and vigorous—and it is becoming possible to recognize the works of individual masters.

The plaque shown here represents the sacrifice of a bull. It is in comparatively high relief, which gives the depth needed for strong shadow. In spite of the frontal position of all but one minor attendant, the composition gives a great sense of movement, emphasized by the contrasting rigidity of the dead animal.

Plaque. Benin. Nigeria. Bronze, height 16¹/₂″. The British Museum, London

Funerary screen. Ijo. Calabar. Wood and cane, height 38⅝″. The British Museum, London

The Ijo funerary screen might be regarded as a proletarian equivalent of the Benin royal plaque. It is, in fact, a funerary screen for the deceased head of a trading concern. Made in the nineteenth century, it is a memorial in his honor, just as was the plaque showing the prestige of the Oba of Benin.

It might also be considered an early forerunner of the technological age, for it was constructed from prefabricated heads, limbs, bodies, and weapons knocked together and set on a background of cane at the time when Western carpentry had been introduced and was becoming popular.

The Tusi screen, used to partition off the platform on which the almost-sacred milkpots stood within the hut, is of traditional craftsmanship, beautifully made, and of excellent design.

Hut screen. Tusi. Rwanda. Reed and cane, height 47¼″. Collection Margaret Trowell, Salisbury, England

Wall painting (detail). Bangba. Northern Congo. Ocher, kaolin, and charcoal. *In situ* Ekibondo Village

Altarpiece for the Yam spirit, Ifijioku. Kwale Ibo. Nigeria. Terra cotta, height 18⁷/₈″. The British Museum, London

The traditional craft of wall painting was revived here many years ago by the then District Commissioner. The central motif represents the sun, the vertical bands the moon, and the undulating lines "the feet of the moon."

In the altarpiece, the head of the family is seen with his wives. In front is his personal shrine *(ikenga)* and the fowl which he is about to sacrifice. The heads of the figures are extremely realistic, and the whole group is full of vitality.

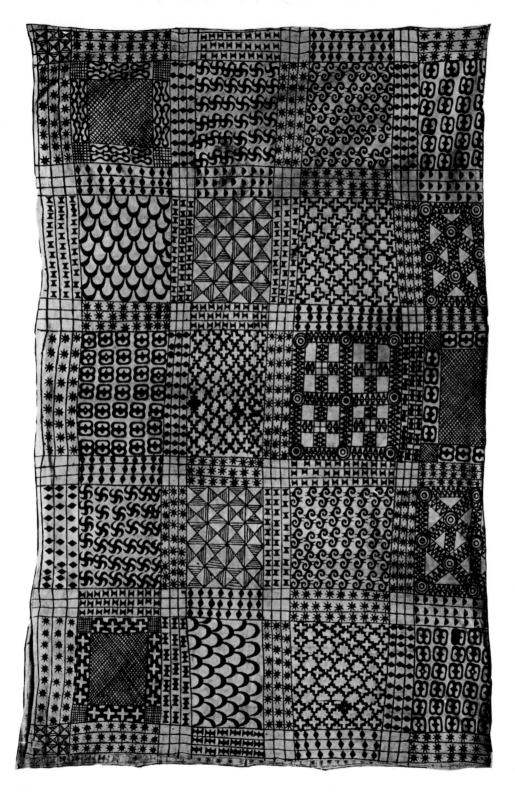

African tribes decorate their textiles in many different ways. The first shown here is an Adinkira cloth, printed in black dye with various small stamps cut from pieces of calabash.

The Bakuba cloth is of loosely woven coarse raffia, the raised parts being further embroidered with finely shredded raffia, which is cut off close to the woven surface forming a texture like pile velvet.

◀ Printed Adinkira textile. Ashanti. Ghana. The British Museum, London

Pile cloth. Bakuba. Congo. Woven and embroidered raffia. Musée Royal de l'Afrique Centrale, Tervueren, Belgium

Printed textile. Bambara. Mali. Cloth dyed and printed with local materials. The British Museum, London

The Bambara, although a most unsophisticated tribe, print their textiles by a complicated chemical discharge method. The cloth is first dyed all over by soaking it in a concoction of bark, and the design is then painted on in mud which probably contains iron acetate. The design is again painted over with a local soap made from ashes and oils containing potash, which acts as a mordant, and finally painted again with the mud used

Woven silk Kente cloth.
Ashanti. Ghana. The
British Museum, London

in the first coat, then dried in the sun. When the mud has been chipped off, the pattern is shown light on a dark ground.

This cloth is made of silk strips, woven on a narrow loom and then sewn together.

Loom heddle pulley. Guro. Ivory Coast. Wood, height 9¹/₂″. Collection Kamer, Cannes

Loom heddle pulley. Baule. Ivory Coast. Wood, height 9¹/₂″. Collection Pierre Vérité, Paris

Loom heddle pulley. Baule. Ivory Coast. Wood, height 8⁵/₈″. Collection Pierre Vérité, Paris

SMALLER ARTIFACTS

Pulleys used to raise and lower the warp heddles of the narrow looms of the Guinea Coast are carved in this attractive way, especially by the Baule and Guro. Even in such small-scale pieces, the tribal characteristics of the work are clearly distinguishable.

Pipe head. Cameroon Grasslands. Bronze, height 9¹/₂″. Collection Tristan Tzara, Paris

Again the aesthetic characteristics of the tribe are expressed in a comparatively small-scale artifact. The typical rough peasant humor of Cameroon carving comes out in the group of small heads at the top of the pipe.

The Bakuba make many wooden cups in the form of human full-sized figures and part figures. The types vary from district to district and from grade to grade within the many different societies which use them for ceremonial drinking.

The beautiful cast-brass jar is a *kuduo,* a ceremonial vessel used at funerals and placed in graves and in the royal mausoleum of Ashanti.

Palm wine cup. Bakuba. Congo. Wood, height 7¹/₂″. Musée de l'Homme, Paris

Kuduo vessel. Ashanti. Ghana. Cast brass, height 13″. Ethnological Collection, Zurich

Ceremonial vessel to hold the wine poured over the royal Golden Stool. Ashanti. Ghana. Terra cotta. The British Museum, London

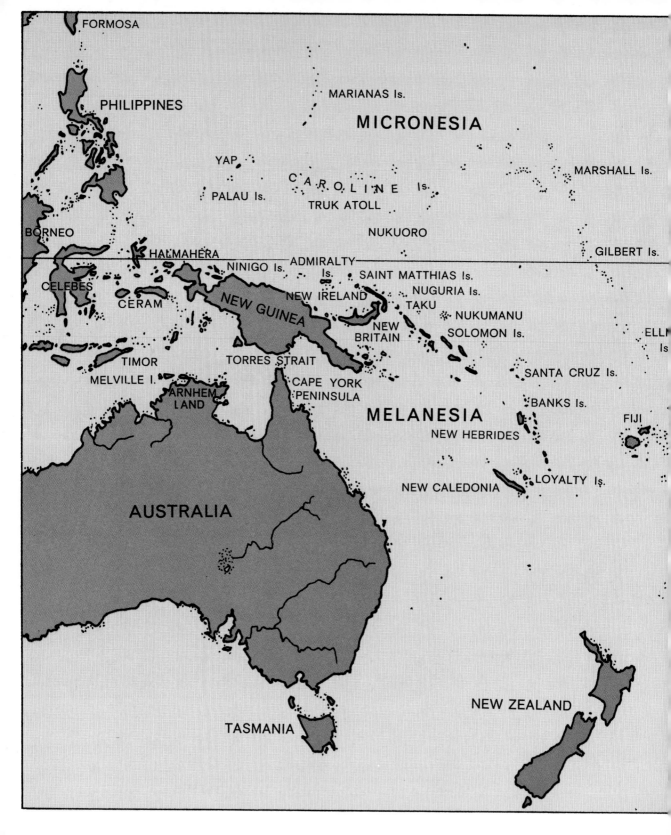

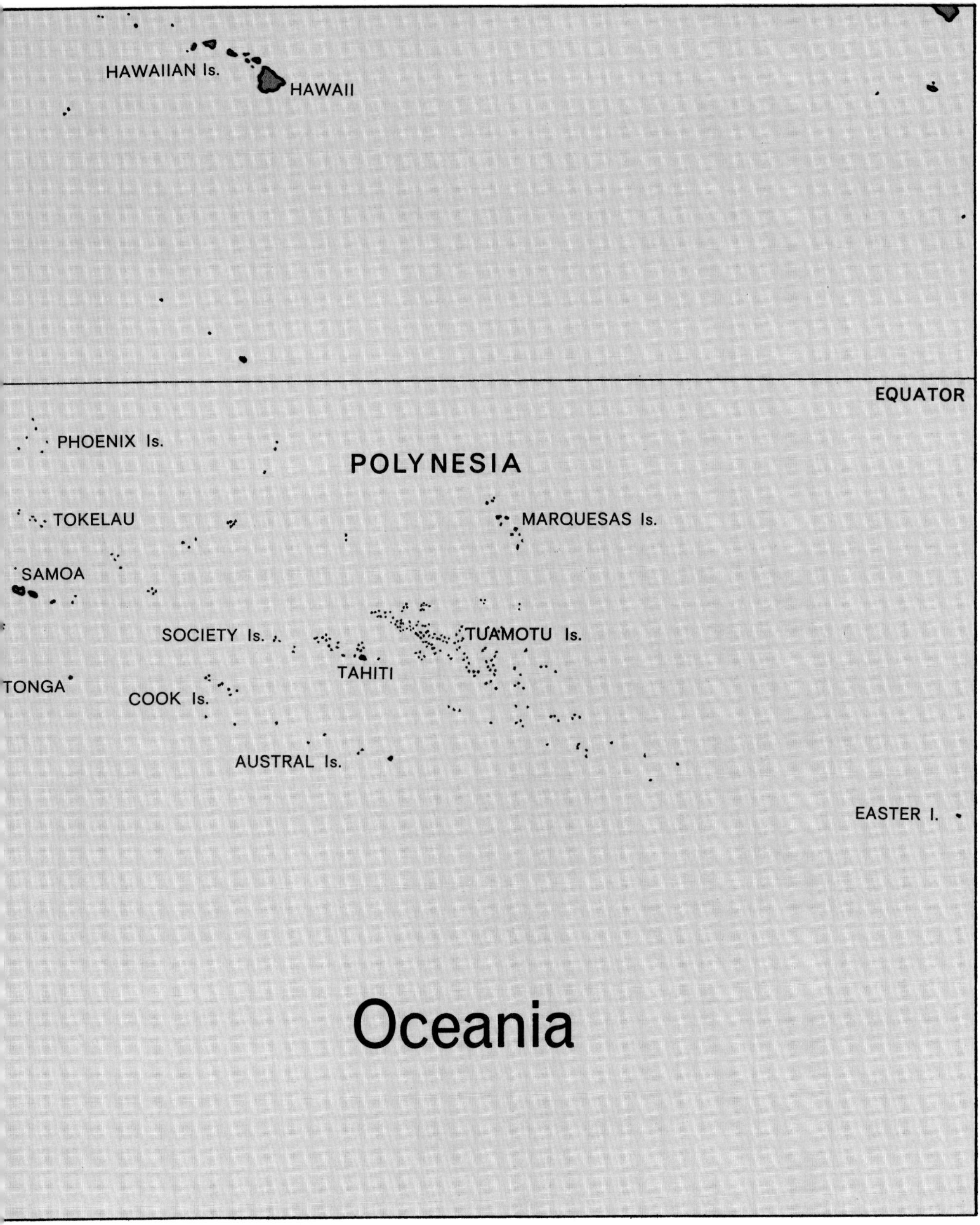

HAWAIIAN Is.

HAWAII

EQUATOR

PHOENIX Is.

POLYNESIA

TOKELAU

MARQUESAS Is.

SAMOA

SOCIETY Is.

TUAMOTU Is.

TAHITI

TONGA

COOK Is.

AUSTRAL Is.

EASTER I.

Oceania

PART TWO:

THE ART OF OCEANIA

TEXT BY HANS NEVERMANN

Diversified as are the forms that art has taken in the many islands of Oceania, and even within the individual regions of such larger areas as New Guinea and Melanesia, there are nevertheless three things they all have in common: a technical development corresponding to that of our Late Stone Age, the fact that artists' names are not known, and a firm connection with a religion which dominates all aspects of daily life.

Except for painting on beaten, not woven, materials such as bark cloth and on the base of large palm-leaf shafts, art in the islands means chiefly sculpture, usually in wood, although, in Polynesia in particular, also in stone. The natives of Oceania remained in the Stone Age until men from the outside world introduced iron implements. But this does not justify considering them backward, since such metals were simply not to be found on most of the islands. For rough work on wood, a curved ax with a horizontally set stone blade sufficed (this was so in the past but not now). Finer work was done with knife-sharp shark teeth, shell splinters, drills with sea-urchin spines, files made of shark's or ray's skin, or at times with bits of obsidian and other natural materials. Obviously the work took much longer than with more highly developed tools, but once a large piece of wood was prepared by rough cutting, usually lengthwise to prevent too rapid drying and resultant splitting, the tedious, slow effort of the final carving of the object was done with loving care and genuine concern.

The individual entrusted with making the work of art was important, at least at the time it was done. In Oceania, as elsewhere, there were the talented and the untalented. But the artist's name was soon forgotten, and what mattered was only the religious significance of the object. This certainly does not mean that the personality and experience of the artist did not count for much. In northern New Ireland, for example, the carvers worked in hidden places, were subject to numerous taboos, and were brought their food by men wearing bird masks.

Religion, as these island people thought of it, must be understood in the broadest sense of the word. Along with the cult of the gods as practiced in Polynesia, for which images of the gods and their symbols were required, Micronesia and the peripheral regions of Polynesia also carried on hero worship, mostly for the leaders of the ancient migrations. In Melanesia, including New Guinea, there was an important ancestor cult, and in the same region the men were—and often still are—organized in secret societies dedicated to the demonlike beings of the earliest creation, who assumed the appearance of men or animals. It is in these cult groups that the use of masks flourishes and in which the decoration of ceremonial huts or places and of cult objects has produced a high level of art. This is particularly true of many areas, such as the Sepik River and its confluents in New Guinea, whose importance was unsuspected before recent explorations.

For these peoples, many things are influenced or determined by religion which, to the outsider, scarcely seem to have any apparent connection with it. Thus, on spears in the northern Solomon Islands, there are small squatting figures rubbed with lime, which are often so simplified as to seem purely ornamental. Yet the Solomon Islanders maintain that without those figures, which they awaken to life by rubbing before a war campaign, the spear would never strike its mark. Similarly, animal figures on boats or eating utensils commonly have magical functions and are not merely decorative. Most often the outsider cannot grasp their meaning, and in places that have become Europeanized too rapidly it may never be known, since often today the lore of their forefathers is no longer passed on to the new generations. The true meaning of many decorative motifs was lost even before the foreigners came, but at least the form in which they are perpetuated is traditional. None the less, one must beware of suspecting religious significance in every tiny ornament. A simple incised notched line in what might be termed a shark's-tooth pattern may well have been handed down as a nonreligious, purely decorative pattern, and often no more than the dislike for an empty space may account for it.

It is not possible to write a history of the art of Oceania, least of all for its western parts—Melanesia and Micronesia—because our acquaintance with them is too recent. Historically, we know only the period of decadence, which began when the ancient religious way of life disappeared and when new tools and colors were introduced, leading to slovenly ways of working and to a deterioration of taste. True enough, in certain areas of New Guinea finds have been made of very ancient small stone figures or stone vessels with figured decoration. But such objects, dug out of the soil, have no connection with the present-day population, who employ them solely for magical purposes and themselves simply do not understand what those stone mortars and pestles were used for. The same is true of Polynesia, although there oral tradition plays a very much greater role. Art objects from the time of the first explorers, that is, from the end of the eighteenth century, are now considered to be rare treasures, and with few exceptions even old stone statues have been valued too highly. In the Marquesas Islands, for example, the very earliest stone images date back only to the eighteenth century, and no wooden sculpture of that period can possibly have survived in such a climate, to say nothing of the even damper tropical forests of Melanesia. If many of the stone monuments on Easter Island must be conceded to be much older, this does not mean that that island was populated earlier than other islands and archipelagoes of Polynesia, or that there was some non-Polynesian influence. The fact is that, despite all the fantastic explanations that have been dreamed up, Easter Island was settled in the twelfth century by Polynesians who probably came from Mangareva and the Marquesas Islands. The lack of wood, combined with a native feeling for the colossal, are sufficient to explain the giant statues of Easter Island which, in terms of artistic quality, are far inferior to the art of the Marquesas.

There is one phenomenon which to date remains unexplained. Despite the vast area it embraces, Polynesia has a relatively unified culture. Ethnographically, it stretches from Hawaii to New Zealand. Its speech and its religion, which made gods out of its ruling aristocracy, suggest a common origin for all of Polynesia despite many local variants. There were even the beginnings of a loose confederation of states with a common holy place on Ra'iatea near Tahiti. And yet, in spite of all this, Polynesia never developed a uniform art. In the first regions to be settled—Samoa and Tonga—there is not even sculpture other than tiny figures carved from sperm-whale teeth on Tonga. But everywhere else in Polynesia, whose central core became the Society Islands (French Oceania) around A.D. 750, there was a notable development of wood carving and often also of stone carving, though almost always in a diversity of local styles. Probably this first occurred in the second great epoch of Polynesian sea voyages, in the twelfth century or later. The earliest date we can give for the development of the special style of New Zealand is the period after 1350, when a great mass of new settlers came there from the Society and Cook Islands. Before then, New Zealand was inhabited only by a small group of early Polynesians of a much lower cultural level.

For Melanesia we have no such dates. Although ancestor worship plays a great role there—and not only the ancestors of the chiefs but also those of each family—memory does not reach back very far, in the best of cases no more than two generations, and it is notable that Melanesian society is split into small, even tiny groups. Even moderately large islands are inhabited by several different tribes, who not only view the others with enmity but also speak different dialects and even different languages. On New Guinea, the tribes and languages are counted in the hundreds, and in the coastal areas, side by side with Melanesian languages, there are also the entirely different tongues which have been designated as Papuan. In spite of these many differences, it must be kept in mind that changes in religious art have not taken place with any degree of rapidity, since the basic cast of mind of these people is extremely conservative. This is especially apparent in the art of the secret societies, whose rituals take place with punctilious and even pedantic respect for the ancient precepts, as shown by the fact that they usually concern events of the most primeval times and their magical re-enactment. If, for example, it is desired to recount the creation of fire, food, social institutions, or the like by means of songs, masks, and a kind of simple dramatic action, everything must be executed strictly according to the old rites if the great events of the earliest times are to be infused, to some extent at least, with new force. If errors creep in, or if there are willful deviations from the ancient tradition, there is the risk that some dire harm will befall the basic needs of man, and that must be avoided at all costs. This is especially true of the festivities associated with the initiation of boys into manhood. Even small mistakes in the decoration of the ritual accessories can bring that about. It is obvious from this that the old forms have survived through the ages, and that changes creep in only gradually and unnoticed, certainly in no case deliberately.

It is a mistake to describe the masks worn in such ceremonies as dance masks exclusively, as is often done. Certainly many masks are associated with dances, but others, such as those of the Kiwai of Papua in British New Guinea, represent the dead and are displayed before the onlookers during a solemn procession. Those of the Marind-anim in West Irian (former Dutch New Guinea) are more accurately described as headdresses than as masks. They are worn during the initiation ceremonies of the men's secret societies to intensify the dramatic effect of the appearance of the primeval demons. But, above all, in Melanesia masks are never mere adornment unless the community has sadly degenerated. They are cult figures held to be the seat of a supernatural creature who takes possession of the wearer: the man who puts on the mask is no longer simply a man in costume but is himself the actual spirit of the dead or a demon.

Outside of Melanesia masks are rare. In Micronesia they are found only on the Mortlock Atoll. At the time of the first foreign explorations there was only one kind of mask in Tahiti, and it represented a death demon. The entire attitude toward masks as cult objects is different in Polynesia from that in Melanesia. In the latter they are taken to be the permanent dwelling of a supernatural being, whereas in Polynesia they are believed to be such a dwelling potentially only, the divinity being summoned forth by rituals and then taking his place in the mask, from which he must be dismissed before the ceremonial taboos are lifted. In Hawaii, however, the making of an image of a god could assume special significance if accompanied by a human sacrifice.

A peculiarity of Melanesia is the connection between certain types of image and specific kinship and settlement groups, and this is associated with totemism. Mostly this involves representations of animals in masks, statues, cult objects, and the like, and outsiders are forbidden to make use of such things. Only a person who through his origins stands in a special relationship to the primeval being represented in animal form may assume the role of that being, sing his songs, and perform the special functions appropriate to it. In the Bismarck Archipelago, on New Britain and New Ireland, the rule is not, however, respected. There, there is an attitude rather like that of "copyright," but it does not concern the artist—only the person who commissions the artist to make the image. The "patron" can purchase from the "owner" of a particular figure the right to imitate it, as long as no totemistic law is infringed. The shell money used to acquire that right is not, however, a mere means of payment but rather itself has a magical character. The new person thus empowered even has the right to introduce minor variations into the already over-rich decoration. The style of the figures must always remain unchanged, but the trimmings, so to speak, can be varied. Perhaps this is the way in which, slowly through the centuries, the great diversity of Melanesian art has come about. But New Ireland is an exceptional case, and its art constitutes a special type which, it has often been claimed, goes back to extra-Oceanian influences, though this remains to be proven.

It is also highly unlikely that the northeastern New Guinea masks and figures with a long nose curled up at the end really do derive from images of the Hindu elephant-god Ganesha, since there are absolutely no connecting links with Hindu-Javanese sculpture, least of all in eastern Indonesia and western New Guinea. On the other hand, the so-called Korwar figures of northwestern New Guinea, squatting human figures with cubical faces and horizontally cut-off chins, do have both a geographical and a technical connection with statues in the small islands of eastern Indonesia, which likewise are used in ancestor worship.

Finally, for all the conservatism of Oceania, reciprocal influences between regions cannot be ruled out. Small carvings from the teeth of sperm whales are made only by the early Polynesian Tongans and by the Fijis, who were originally Melanesian but were colonized by the Tongans. In the Admiralty Islands the gourd flasks used for the chalk chewed along with betel have a very different type of decoration from that on their wood carvings, but it is similar to that done in the Hermit Islands. In northeastern New Guinea, groups which speak the quite different Melanesian and Papuan languages nevertheless have a common religion and a common style in art.

For Melanesia, the Basel ethnologist Felix Speiser has proposed a system of stylistic categories based on certain broad distinctions. Thus, after a somewhat vague "Primary Style," he names the various styles either according to external traits, so that we get the Curved and Beaked Styles, or after the principal sites, such as Tami Style (after small islands near eastern New Guinea), or after certain local manifestations, such as the Malanggan Style of New Ireland and the Korwar Style of Dutch New Guinea. This seems a much needed means of bringing order into such a multiplicity of phenomena. But much more work will have to be done to get a clear picture of the styles in relation to other factors—such as the material cultural conditions, sociology, anthropology, traditions of migrations, forms of worship, and so forth—the more so since thoroughgoing research is still lacking for many tribes and is in fact no longer feasible for them, as for many others that have now been subjected to European influences which no doubt work to their economic and social advantage but certainly do nothing for their art.

Further, these stylistic categories cannot be applied to all of Oceania. One cannot simply connect the Curved Style of New Guinea with the Spiral Style of New Zealand, especially since there is no evidence of a pre-Polynesian settlement of New Zealand. The same applies to the attempt to relate the depictions of frigate birds in the Solomon Islands to those of Easter Island. After all, how else can one depict a frigate bird than with a long hooked beak? Here the prototype is everything, the subsequent imitations nothing. For the time being, we can set up only one group for Polynesia, that embracing both the Society and Austral Islands, but that, in the face of all the other separate developments, is very little. What, however, does unite many Polynesian peoples is their masterly skill in stone carving for religious purposes, that is, for places of worship and foundations for houses and tombs, and this is found all the way from Tonga to the Marquesas Islands and Easter Island. But along with this there is also a crude, megalithic kind of work which seems to have come from some place far to the west.

If we leave out of consideration Micronesia and the Fiji Islands, which are poor in art, there are still two fundamental differences between Melanesian and Polynesian art. The art of Polynesia is determined by the cult of the high gods and of the chieftains who allegedly descend from them. It is, therefore, "aristocratic" in orientation and characteristic of a people who were developing into a civilized nation but whose development was cut short by intervention from outside. In contrast, Melanesian art is based on ancestor worship, totemism, and other religious concepts, but never on chieftains who, in fact, do not even exist in many places. It is, instead, the expression of men living close to the soil. It is a "peasant" art based on the thinking of small sedentary communities, whereas that of the Polynesians, extremely skillful seafarers, is more grandiose in conception. This explains the Melanesians' delight in bright colors—red and sometimes yellow made from earths, white from lime, black from soot or mud, but never blue or green (except for the Sulkas on New Britain, who use green as a supplement to red). Compared with that of Africa, Melanesian art is exceptionally colorful. On the other hand, Polynesian art prefers the aristocratic use of fine woods, places value on beautiful graining, and rejects bright colors. Of the innate good taste of the Polynesians, scarcely anything more significant can be said than that they are one of the few peoples on earth who openly enjoy beautiful landscapes in the same way as the Eastern Asians and the Europeans—and the latter learned to do so only in the Renaissance.

It is common to all of Oceania that never was there any effort to achieve anything like the classical ideal of Antiquity of Western civilization. Certainly the proportions in their wooden or stone statues are generally erroneous, and the head especially is too large for the body and the body too large for the legs, but that is something which has never disturbed anyone. The concept of beauty never became fully fixed in Oceania, and often it is emotional expression which weights the scale to one side or the other. If the face painting or tattooing is carried out correctly ("tattooing" takes its name from the Polynesian *tatau*), people are perfectly content with the mask or figure, even if everything else about it seems out of keeping according to our notions. Never anywhere in Oceania has an art object, even the simplest ornament, been made for the sake of its beauty. A work of art in and for itself would be for all the inhabitants of Oceania, for dark-skinned Melanesians and light-colored Polynesians alike, simply an absurdity. Feeling and religious relevance are all that matter.

This relevance was blithely ignored when Europe became acquainted with "South Sea art," first through Paul Gauguin, and then again in the 1920s, when it was rediscovered along with African art and hailed as a true art. It is significant that even artists like Gauguin and Pechstein, who themselves lived and painted in Oceania, found no real personal relationship with Oceanian art and, for all their progressive ideals, could never slough off their own European attitudes. Nor is it enough to be "primitive" or even more, like Picasso, to wish to be, because the Oceanians are in no way primitive, but are, rather, a people with their own beliefs and traditions. True, one can imitate their forms, and no one can deny an artist's right to do so. But without understanding their lore, their beliefs, and their rigid ties to an ancient tradition, every attempt to imitate their art must inevitably prove futile. If today all Polynesians and so many Melanesians are already no longer bound to their ancient traditions, how can an outsider dare hope to match their ancient art?

The Papuan-speaking inhabitants of the Ramu and Sepik river valleys believe, like most Papuans and Melanesians, that a man has many souls. Some souls appear to him in dreams and visions, others linger for a while at his grave before finally disappearing into the realm of the dead, still others live on, unseen, near his descendants. As dwellings for the last-named kind of soul, small figures are carved which range in height from three inches to three feet. They are streaked with reddish-brown pigment, the color of blood and life, to assure the continued existence of the soul. Usually they are kept in the men's house or in what we would call a temple. But they may be given over to a man wise in magic, or else, if very small, worn as a talisman even when the name of the ancestor has been long forgotten.

Ancestor figure, from the Ramu River delta, northeastern New Guinea. Wood, height $7^1/_2''$. Rautenstrauch-Joest Museum, Cologne

For coarser work such as felling trees or rough shaping of wooden images, canoes, drums, and the like, in Oceania an ax is used whose shaft is made from the trunk of a tree, the haft from a stout branch. A stone blade of neolithic type is tied to the end of the shaft, its cutting edge set at an angle. In Polynesia the over-all form is rectangular, in Melanesia lancet-shaped. Different from these utility axes

Ritual ax without blade, from the Ramu River delta, northeastern New Guinea. Wood, length of haft $21^5/_8''$, of shaft $16^7/_8''$. Rautenstrauch-Joest Museum, Cologne

are others which are lovingly decorated and used in religious rites, most often those connected with the initiation of boys or their admission into the men's society, generally one and the same ceremony. In these rites they symbolize the discovery of man's cultural values by the ancient heroes, though they may also typify other mythological themes. However, they are not in themselves symbols of a god, as are the ritual axes of the Polynesian Cook Islands, where they represent Tane, the god of handicrafts.

Headrest, from the northeastern coast of New Guinea, region of Dallmannhafen. Wood, $6^1/_2 \times 7^1/_4''$.
Rautenstrauch-Joest Museum, Cologne

To protect the often highly elaborate coiffures of their woolly hair, Melanesians, like natives of many parts
of Africa, often sleep with the lower part of the back of the head, but not the neck, resting on a small carved
support which is concave on top and has legs made of thin bamboo, or else may be entirely carved out of
a single block of wood. For all that these are ordinary utility objects, they are generally combined with
ancestor figures, because dreams are taken to be true experiences during which one may have need of an
ancestor's protection. That is why these objects are also painted with bright, life-stimulating colors, to keep
the guardian-ancestors alert.

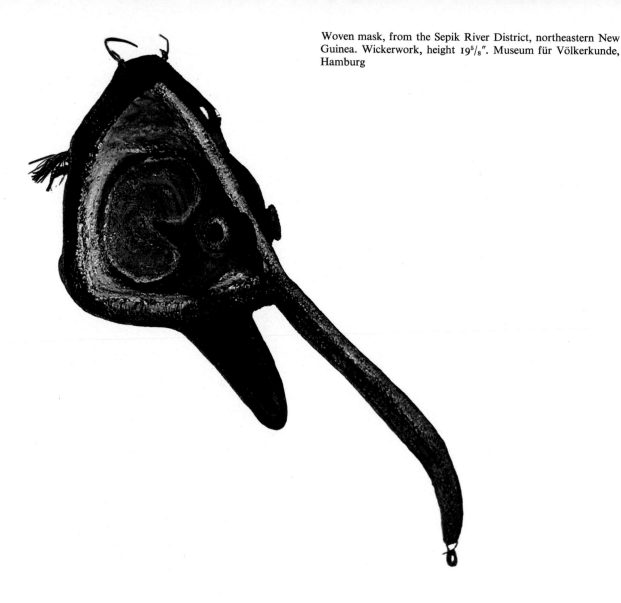

Woven mask, from the Sepik River District, northeastern New Guinea. Wickerwork, height 19⅝″. Museum für Völkerkunde, Hamburg

When the Sepik River valley was explored in 1912, it was a great surprise to find that it was inhabited by an as yet undisturbed people with an art of the utmost significance. There are often quite distinct styles demarcated by the river's lower and middle courses and tributaries. Among the Iatmul people especially, wickerwork masks were found in addition to the predominant wood carvings. They were, however, relatively rare, since they could be worn only by the leaders of the ceremonies of initiation into manhood. The long nose frequently found on these masks appears also on wooden masks.

Mask, from the Sepik River District, northeastern New Guinea. Painted wood, height 9¹/₂". Koninklijk Instituut voor de Tropen, Amsterdam

On close inspection, the Sepik River masks often seem not to be masks at all, since they have no holes for the eyes. They were not tied directly over the face, however, but were instead attached to a wickerwork base drawn over the head; it is possible to see through the interstices of the basketry. The man who wore such a mask was presumed to be possessed by the power of the spirit represented, and he himself felt that he had become the actual spirit or demon of primeval times. These masks also were closely connected with the rites of initiation into manhood, and always represent beings who stand in a mythical kinship relationship to a group of a particular descent or locality.

Mask, from the Sepik River District, north-eastern New Guinea. Painted wood, height $33^{1}/_{8}''$. Koninklijk Instituut voor de Tropen, Amsterdam

In contrast to the Sepik and Ramu delta regions, where carvings are painted simply with just a red-earth color, farther inland in the Sepik Valley, up to the end of the river's middle course and along its tributaries, the people delight in bright painting in red, white, and black. Here the Curved Style dominates. Straight lines are almost superstitiously avoided, and the style is based on circles, often one within another, or on arcs which may flow into one another. Typical also is the breadth of the face, round eyes, often also round spots on the cheeks, and little emphasis on the nose. What counts always is the head itself. The rest of the body, if depicted at all, is merely incidental, and consequently, as with so many primitive peoples, is of excessively reduced proportions.

In the Sepik region, the artist cannot simply vary the painting of a mask at will. He must keep to the designs worn by the dead man during his lifetime. Those were the dead man's personal property, as it were, and not to be imitated by others. Spirits and demons likewise have their own personal, immutable designs. This has nothing to do with the proportions of a mask, which are subject to variation. If the skulls modeled over with clay which are found in this region strike foreign observers as portraitlike, that is not in itself the determining factor for the Iatmul and other New Guinea peoples; what is essential is only the personal design. If that is correct, then it can be used even on an exaggeratedly elongated head or on a face an observer from outside would consider far from lifelike, and the individual "portrayed" would still be recognizable.

Two jars decorated with pigs' heads, from the central Sepik River District, northeastern New Guinea. Painted earthenware, height of left jar 32¼". Museum für Völkerkunde, Berlin

Some localities along the southern tributaries of the Sepik make pottery, though naturally without a potter's wheel. Their products came to be distributed far and wide through barter. Typically they are shallow cone-shaped eating vessels with incised decoration on the underside, but there are also high-necked vessels which were placed on roofs at the end of the high ridgepole, for both decoration and protection. Besides these, alrge jars were made for storing sago meal and mash. The pig's head modeled in relief on the necks of the jars seen here represents a primeval demon who plays a role in the mythology of the totem groups. It was he who created the means of nourishment for the first men, so now he must watch that the food for festive occasions is abundant and does not spoil.

Masks, from the Sepik River District, north-eastern New Guinea. Painted wood with ornaments added, height of the larger mask 25$^{1}/_{4}$″. Koninklijk Instituut voor de Tropen, Amsterdam

Along the lower course of the Sepik the Beaked Style predominates, but along the middle course it is joined by the Curved Style, so that there both styles exist side by side. In the Beaked Style, verticals are emphasized. Even the eyes are set slanting upward, and the nose, or a projection coming off below it, is extended downward like a beak or trunk; its lower end is either free-hanging or else curves to join the navel or genitals. It has been proposed that these projections have something to do with notions as to the origin of life, but at this early stage of research into the spiritual concepts of the Sepik people we cannot be certain of that. Again it is the correctly painted designs, not the proportions, which permit identification with particular ancestors or demons. Many of the masks are further decorated with hair from a dead man in order to make their magic more potent. Often there is ornamentation with sea-snail shells pressed into resin or wax. The blue coloring seen here, as a rule a sign of a degenerating art, points to a time in which European sailors still used bluing for their laundry, that is, before 1914.

Gable ornament with figure surmounted by a sea eagle, from central Sepik River District, northeastern New Guinea. Wood, height 40¹/₂". Museum für Völkerkunde, Berlin

The Sepik Valley villages have men's houses whose projecting, high-towering gables raise them above the mass of smaller houses for women and children, which the men visit only occasionally. The prominence of the men's houses leaves no doubt that they are the central point of the religious and social life of the men. If a village is inhabited by different settlement or totem groups, there will be several such houses. The front gable is usually decorated with a statue of a sea eagle as symbol of the warlike character of the men who live there. When the eagle surmounts a human figure, which stands for the mythical founder of the house and of the rites which take place in it, it also represents the soul-bird which carried the founding father into the other world and will do the same for the house's present occupants. Copies of such birds are made of baked clay and are set up at the ends of the ridgepoles as protection against the tropical rains, but they are usually much inferior to the wood-carved originals in both size and expressiveness.

Carved hanger, from Sepik River District, north-eastern New Guinea. Wood, height 37". Rautenstrauch-Joest Museum, Cologne

In the region of the Curved Style, but also extending into that of the Beaked Style, there are also figures carved in low relief on one side only. These resemble the ancestor and demon figures of the locality, but beneath their feet they have a crescent-shaped projection ending to either side in a hook. They are used to hang nets or baskets with food in them out of reach of dogs and rats. The supernatural creature represented, identifiable sometimes by the hair added but always by the facial painting, is therefore at one and the same time a cult object and a useful device for protecting the provisions which, if kept in the men's houses, are destined for the ritual meal in which the participants enter into communion with their forefathers.

House panel, from Tami Islands, northeastern New Guinea. Painted wood, 28³/₄″. Rautenstrauch-Joest Museum, Cologne

The Tami Style takes its name from the small islands off the coast at Finschhafen. It is characterized by sobriety, right-angled lines, rectangular faces which are flat and taper down somewhat below, large headdresses, and the absence of the neck, which makes the heads seem to sit directly on the chests. Similar traits appear in the serpents, fish, and other creatures which are depicted in reliefs. Although the Tamis' long wooden bowls are entirely black except for reliefs and incised designs accentuated by rubbed-in chalk, lively coloring in red, white, and black is used for horizontal house panels, headrests, hangers, and boat ornaments. Often the coloring seems added to make up for certain deficiencies in plastic modeling. Also very popular here are depictions of serpents and of men being swallowed by snakes or crocodiles, perhaps in association with the idea of death and rebirth in the ritual of initiation into manhood. On the back of this house panel is an ancestor figure in relief.

Mask, from the Papua Gulf, southern New Guinea. Bark cloth over basketry, height $31^{1}/_{2}''$. Museum für Völkerkunde, Hamburg

In the Papua Gulf region of what was formerly British New Guinea, now Papua, cloth is made of the fiber under the bark of certain trees of the fig family. The bark is dampened and beaten to form large sheets of cloth which hold together without being woven. For masks, a light basketlike framework is made of wickerwork and covered with cloth. The basic color is always white, but strips of fiber cloth dyed red and black are stitched on to enliven the whole. Frequently these masks have projecting, snoutlike mouth parts and ears. They usually represent demons of the rich mythological lore of the gulf peoples, but also recently deceased persons, and are displayed in solemn processions. Depictions of animals are very rare in this region.

Paddle blade, from Asmat, southwestern West Irian (former Dutch New Guinea). Carved wood. Koninklijk Instituut voor de Tropen, Amsterdam

Inaccessible as it is, with swamplands strung along a narrow, forbidding coast, the Asmat region was not opened up until 1952. As in the Sepik Valley, here too was found an art in a still pure form. It has some resemblance to the Curved Style, but to outsiders it seems prone to a somewhat chaotic though harmonious play of line which, except for human and animal figures, tends to be severely stylized. Color is used extensively only on wooden shields. For other objects it is used very sparingly, and because it is easily washed off is not applied at all to boats and paddles. The paddles employed by the men who steer the boats hollowed out of a single tree trunk have very long shafts, whereas those used by the women, who remain seated, are shorter.

The thought of the Asmats centers on head-hunting and the survival of the community. For every man killed by enemy head-hunters, a kind of totem pole is set up, made from a tree trunk and with a decoratively carved shelf at the base, the whole assuming an anthropomorphic form. Before it is laid a "soul boat," carved from a smaller tree trunk, on which are small figures of the year-bird as symbol of the slain warrior, and of a turtle as a fertility symbol. In front of the soul boat the ceremonial scarification in decorative designs of the youths preparing to take their place as men and preservers of the community's fertility takes place. When the ceremony is over, or when the dead man has been avenged, the work of art has fulfilled its purpose and is thrown away into the bush.

Bird figure from a soul boat, from Asmat, southwestern West Irian (former Dutch New Guinea). Length of the whole boat 30′ 2″. Koninklijk Instituut voor de Tropen, Amsterdam

MELANESIA

In the northern part of New Ireland, every year there are great festivals for the dead, for which special figures and masks are made for dead individuals. However, only a single commemorative figure is made for all the deceased chiefs together, and it is quite different in style and less colored. These "Uli" figures are not, as is claimed, hermaphroditic, nor do they have anything to do with the predominant matriarchal system of the island. Rather, they are based on the idea that chiefs become wealthy and well-nourished and are, so to speak, the mothers of the community. While other figures are destroyed after the ceremony, the Uli, which must not be seen by the women, are preserved in houses kept closed up.

Uli figure, from New Ireland, Bismarck Archipelago. Wood, height 57$^1/_8$". Museum für Völkerkunde, Berlin

Mask, from northern New Ireland. Wood and ▶ bark cloth, height 15³/₄". Museum für Völkerkunde, Hamburg

Between southern New Ireland, which is connected culturally with the neighboring area of New Britain, and the northern part, whose art revolves around the Uli figures and the so-called *malanggans,* there is a zone in whose mountains chalk is found. Figures of male and female ancestors are carved in this easily worked material. This is the only stone sculpture in Melanesia other than the sandstone statues in human or animal form which are made in New Britain for the secret society called *ingiet* to represent the soul-bearers of the members, and which are displayed in the ceremonial grounds.

The New Ireland masks decorated with a kind of helmet crest derive from an out-of-date style of hairdress which had formerly been worn as a sign of mourning. They are worn by dancers, whereas other masks, which are done in openwork carving and have large ears attached, represent the dead and are worn only by men who go about collecting shell money as a donation to the festival. Both types of mask are made in strict secrecy but are exhibited openly on festival days and thereafter worn without restriction. The eyes here are made of the greenish shell of a kind of sea snail, the turbo.

Ancestor figure, from central New Ireland. Chalk, height 23⁵/₈". Museum für Völkerkunde, Hamburg

Northern New Ireland is the region of the so-called *malanggans,* large openwork carvings in soft wood, usually in the form of horizontal friezes. These are carved and painted in secrecy by specialized artists and then, on festival days commemorating the dead, the mats concealing them are removed and the *malanggans* are solemnly "unveiled" for public inspection in front of special, roofed-over walls. While the *malanggans* are connected with the commemoration of the dead, their symbolism also includes elements associated with

Malanggan, from northern New Ireland. Wood, length 63″. Museum für Völkerkunde, Hamburg

the moon cult and totemism. Their style is not open to change, but the right to introduce variants in details can be purchased with shell money. As a result, there has come about an accumulation of symbols of the most diverse kinds, almost beyond the comprehension of an outsider. None the less, the most important figures remain traditional: men as the principal figures, wearing white disks of shell on their chests, serpents, flying fishes, year-birds, catfish, and cocks.

Skull mask, from Gunantuna tribe (Tolai), Gazelle ▶
Peninsula, New Britain, Bismarck Archipelago.
Bone and resin, $10^5/_8 \times 6^1/_8$". Rautenstrauch-
Joest Museum, Cologne

Along with the horizontal friezelike *malanggans* are exhibited
vertical *malanggans,* Uli figures, and masks. The festivals at which
they are displayed, also called *malanggans,* have lost much of their
old meaning, and at times resemble nothing more than the opening
of an art exhibition. Whence the fact that in New Ireland a special
problem of aesthetics arises along with the problem of the legiti-
macy of acquiring by purchase the right to introduce variations
in the arrangement of details. Such new variations finally come to
assume greater importance than the traditional meaning of the
individual symbols.

On New Britain, the Gunantuna, who are now officially renamed
Tolai, make masks out of the front part of a skull and jaw, with
soft parts modeled in resin and painted. A stick is attached horizontally to the back, and the wearer grips his teeth on it to hold
on the mask. Any connection with the death cult can no longer be
ascertained today, but such masks formerly served chiefly to
identify those who were charged with dividing up the magic-laden
shell money.

Malanggan, from northern New Ireland. Wood,
height $51^1/_8$". Museum für Völkerkunde, Hamburg

Sheath mask, from Sulka tribe, New Britain. Basketry and pith, height without grass skirt 31$^1/_2$". Museum für Völkerkunde, Hamburg

The Sulka masks are made of a rattan with flexible stems, onto which strips of tree pith are sewn. They are painted dark red and, for decoration, streaked with black and green, the latter color being entirely exceptional in the South Seas. They are pulled on over the head and worn in public processions to bring health and growth to the uninitiated, that is, to women and children.

Cloth mask, from Baining tribe, Gazelle Peninsula, New Britain. Bark cloth on basketry frame, height 33$\frac{1}{2}$". Museum für Völkerkunde, Hamburg

In the hinterland of the Gazelle Peninsula in New Britain lives the Baining tribe, which originated in that region. Unlike their Melanesian neighbors, they speak a Papuan language and have no secret societies. Masks are not hidden from women and are closely associated with the fertility of humans, domesticated animals (pigs), and food plants. They are made of bark cloth drawn over basketlike wickerwork frames and decorated with black designs. After the processional display of the masks, which are often gigantic in size, the spectators rip off pieces of cloth to bury in their fields as a magical means of guaranteeing fertility.

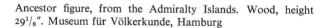
Ancestor figure, from the Admiralty Islands. Wood, height 29⅛″. Museum für Völkerkunde, Hamburg

The religion of the Admiralty Islands people is entirely based on veneration of personal, benevolent ancestors, among whom it is the most recently dead who are the most highly honored. The soul is thought to continue to reside in the skull of the dead man which is kept in the family house, or in a wooden figure always painted red and which wears an old-fashioned tuftlike hairdress.

Guardian figure for a boat, from the central Solomon Islands. Wood, height 11³/₄". Museum für Völkerkunde, Berlin

The boats of most of the South Sea Islanders are carved from a single tree trunk and have a long outrigger beam attached alongside to prevent tipping over. But the Solomon Islanders build large, seaworthy boats of planks, with high bow and sternpost, generally painted black. On the bow, somewhat above the waterline, a small statue is attached, which consists only of a head with protruding lips and with supporting arms. Its function is to keep a sharp watch and drive away sea spirits which might bring storms. The protruding mouth is related to this notion and in no way resembles the physical type of the Melanesians.

Fish figure, from the southern Solomon Islands. Wood
with mother-of-pearl inlay, length 80³/₄". The British
Museum, London

In the thinking of the inhabitants of the central and southern Solomon Islands, a special role is played by the
spirits of sharks, serpents, and dead warriors. The serpent-spirits protect the plantings, the shark-spirits keep
seafarers from harm. A peculiarity of the southern Solomon Islanders is decoration of black-painted wooden
objects such as bowls, net-floats, and human and animal figures with inlays of white shell fragments pains-
takingly cut out with Stone Age implements.

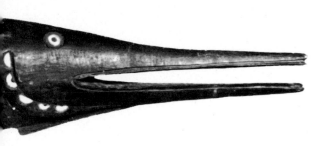

Door panel, from New Caledonia. Wood, height 82¼". Museum für ▶
Völkerkunde, Berlin

On New Caledonia the typical round houses with high conical roofs which serve as dwellings for the chiefs and as cult
centers are crowned, at the highest point, by a stylized figure.
To either side of the door there are also panels with human
figures whose bodies are made of a rhomboid pattern and
whose faces, with their broad, flat noses and wide mouths,
correspond to the New Caledonians' ideal of beauty. These
panels are always made of a durable material, and are usually
given as a gift by the maternal relatives, since they portray the
early ancestors of that side of the family.

Not many masks survive from the northern part of New Caledonia. There they are considered the dwelling of the souls of heroes of the past who wander in from foreign parts and take up residence in a mask. However, the tribes to the south have forgotten the old meaning, and today the few masks existing are put on only to frighten the people. Nevertheless, the masks are for the most part owned by magicians who consider them to possess some sort of power which they themselves can no longer define very precisely. The body is covered by a net into which are stuck blackish-green feathers, and above the wooden face towers a roll of hair made of either real hair or plant fibers.

Mask, from New Caledonia. Wood, wickerwork, hair, and feathers, height without feathers 28". Rautenstrauch-Joest Museum, Cologne

The institution of chieftainship has had to give way in the central and northern New Hebrides to the influence of the *suque,* a men's secret society based on a rigorous hierarchy. In order to rise to the higher grades, sacrifices must be made of domesticated boars whose tusks have been skillfully rounded off, and this demands considerable financial outlay and wealth. Such rank, however, endows a man with personal prestige and magical powers. Only those who have won a high place have the right to install statues in front of their houses as insignia of their rank. Besides wood carvings, there are also statues made from the fibrous trunks of giant ferns.

Insigne of rank, from northern New Hebrides. Fern wood, height 88⅝".
Museum für Völkerkunde, Berlin

Sculpture is very rare in Micronesia. Where it exists, it usually depicts the historical or legendary leaders of the migrations which explored the islands or came from outside as powerful new settlers. Probably the form of this statue owes much to foreign influences, perhaps even European.

Ancestor figure (?), from Tobi, Caroline Islands. Wood painted white, height 15″. Museum für Völkerkunde, Berlin (destroyed)

Gable figure of a bachelors' house, from the Palau
Islands. Wood, 25⁵/₈ × 40¹/₈″. Museum für Völkerkunde, Berlin

Among the few types of free-standing statuary in Micronesia are the figures set up on the gables of the unmarried men's houses. These always portray a woman of high rank, as shown by the large bracelet of dugong
bone she wears; she represents the readiness to conceive of an ancestress. Such houses, made of beams held
together with mortise and tenon joints, have nothing to do with the men's secret society houses of Melanesia.
They are merely dwellings for the unmarried young men, who receive visits there from the marriageable girls.

The gable walls and beams of the bachelors' houses are entirely covered with reliefs. Individual figures are made to stand out in high relief by deeper carving around them. The only colors used are yellow earth for the background plus black and white with, very rarely, some red. The rows of figures illustrate events from mythology, history, and fables, with which the viewer is presumed to be acquainted.

Relief carving on a beam of a bachelors' house, from the Palau Islands. Wood, length 45^1/$_4$″. Museum für Völkerkunde, Hamburg

Mask, from the Mortlock Islands, central Carolines. Wood, $24\frac{1}{4} \times 10\frac{1}{4}''$. Rautenstrauch-Joest Museum, Cologne

The only masks in Micronesia come from the Mortlock Atoll. They have no connection with religious societies but simply portray some benevolent spirit. They are worn during dances on the beach in which the spirit is encouraged to protect the food supply by driving typhoons away from Mortlock.

POLYNESIA

The "Pyramid" of Mahaiatea on Tahiti. Steel engraving from James Wilson, *A Missionary Voyage,* London, 1799

The sanctuaries of Polynesia, the *marae* or *malae* (in Hawaii, *heiau*), were carefully paved with stones and surrounded by walls, and were always kept neat and clean. At one end was a stone altar on which the images of the gods were set up, and in the rest of the space there were monoliths as backrests for those aristocrats who could trace their ancestry back to the gods. The so-called Pyramid of the Mahaiatea district in Tahiti has nothing in common with the pyramids of the Old or New World. It owes its origin to the thirst for power of Queen Purea, who raised an altar to the glory of her son which grew so high that it became a kind of long step-pyramid. It was erected between 1762 and 1768, but after Purea was defeated in a war against the local chieftains, the altar of field stones and blocks of coral soon fell into ruin. The last vestiges were pitilessly destroyed in 1865, when they were used for lime burning and to build a bridge.

Figure of a god, from the Cook Islands. Wood, height 19⁵/₈″. Rautenstrauch-Joest Museum, Cologne

Not many Polynesian statues of gods have survived, because the first explorations were quickly followed by the arrival of missionaries at the end of the eighteenth century. Typical of the Cook Islands are these squat figures with overlarge head and horizontally set eyes. Unlike the usual Polynesian practice, here the figures are sometimes painted. The figure seen here is not one of the major divinities, but more likely a patron-god of fishermen, and was meant to be attached to the bow of a boat like a figurehead in order to guarantee a good catch.

Paddle-shaped sacrificial utensils, from Raivavae, Austral Islands (Tubuai Group). Wood, length of the longest scoop 53⅛". National Museum, Copenhagen

Despite their paddle shape, the so-called ceremonial oars of the Austral Islands were scarcely meant to be used as paddles or even as implements to be carried in dances. They were, instead, used to deposit sacrificial offerings on altars with due reverence. The altars were taboo, and could not be touched by human hands during the ceremonies as long as the gods who had been summoned up might still be present. These sacrificial scoops with carefully worked notch decoration are found on Raivavae Island only. The small human figures on the edge of the handle are called *tiki*. The word generally means little more than "human figure," but may also apply to the first man created by the gods or even to the creator himself who, however, is not reckoned among the greater gods.

The art of the Marquesas Islands is distinguished by rich relief ornamentation and by the round eyes on the anthropomorphic stone and wood statues. This form of the eye imitates the eye socket of the human skull; originally there was a connection with both the ancestor cult and the practice of taking heads as trophies. Such figures appear not only as large statues, but were also used on utility objects in order to increase their power. Thus, this *tiki* on the foot grip of a stilt guarantees to the user victory over his rivals in stilt games.

Stone figure, from the Marquesas Islands. Gray basalt, height 7⁸/₄″. Museum für Völkerkunde, Berlin

The *tikis* of the Marquesas Islands are anthropomorphic figures, both large and small, of ancestors or gods. In the latter case, they are mostly the lesser gods who, in part, are themselves only deified ancestors of the nobility. This is borne out by the round eyes, which recall those of skulls. The functions of the stone *tikis,* once so abundant and now to be found in museums only, were very diverse, ranging from ancestor images to sinkers for fish nets, the latter a function in which they were thought to be especially helpful.

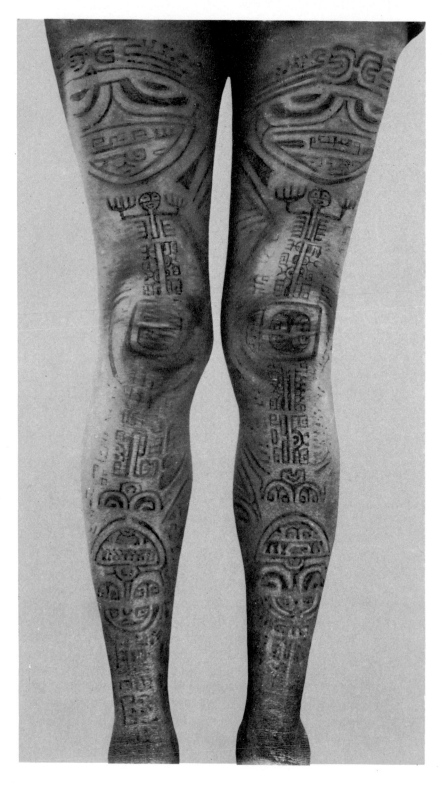

Leg tattoos. Outline drawing of a Marquesas Island design. Museum für Völkerkunde, Berlin. Collection Karl von den Steinen

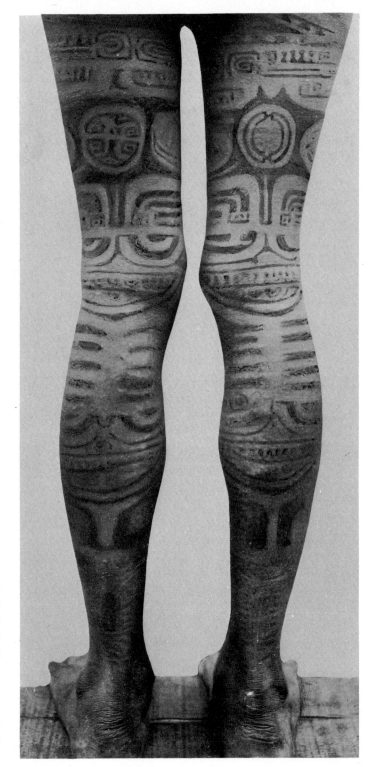

The word "tattoo" comes from the Polynesian *tatau*. The art was practiced throughout Polynesia and in parts of Micronesia, but reached its high point in the Marquesas Islands. There, men's entire bodies were tattooed, a process taking years. The designs were traditional, but were constantly varied in their arrangement. The masters of tattooing were highly respected and occupied the same rank as wood carvers, sculptors, and priests, with whom they shared the title *tuhuna,* master.

Head of the god Kukailimoku. Wickerwork with feathers and human hair, height 21⁵/₈″. Museum für Völkerkunde, Berlin

The goddess Kihevahine, from Hawaii. Kou wood with inlaid human teeth, height 16⁷/₈″. Museum für Völkerkunde, Berlin

The great gods of Polynesia were Tane, creator of the world and lord of crafts; Rongo, lord of the word and of poetry; and the war-god Tu, called in Hawaii Ku or Kukailimoku, "Ku-greedy-for-islands." To them was added later Tangaroa, the god of sea and sky, who took over the role of highest god and creator. This head of the highly venerated Kukaili-moku is made up of a basketry framework over which is drawn a net studded with tiny red feathers. Such feathers are treasured throughout Polynesia: in Hawaii only the highest chiefs may wear feather mantles, and in Tahiti to be arrayed in a girdle of feathers is tantamount to coronation.

The almost animal-like expression of the face of the Hawaiian goddess Kihevahine is in deliberate opposition to the Hawaiian ideal of beauty, which is much like that of Europe. Kihevahine was the goddess of lizards and dragonlike gigantic reptiles. In Hawaii, as throughout Polynesia, there is a great fear of lizards, so that the goddess is thought of also as mistress of other sorts of evil spirits. To make the statue more effective, it originally wore human hair, to which great magical power is ascribed. Characteristic of Hawaii is the way the torso leans forward, particularly at the line of the breasts.

254

House panel with relief, Maori work from New Zealand (detail). Wood, dimensions of detail $33\frac{1}{2} \times 16\frac{7}{8}''$. Museum, Auckland, New Zealand

The New Zealand Polynesians known as Maoris ("natives") emigrated there from the Society and Cook Islands. Once they had exterminated a number of smaller and less highly developed Polynesian groups which had settled there before them, they developed their own style, which has nothing in common with that of their previous homeland. This is seen clearly in the horizontal panels from the houses of chiefs and priests or from special buildings erected to spread the lore of the gods. In these panels the spiral assumes decisive importance. Often a figure is shown flanked by two *manaia,* that is, creatures whose form is composed of the halves of a face seen from the front with, in the middle, a pursed-up mouth; but the halves are separated and presented in side view. Elsewhere in all of Oceania, both humans and gods are shown full-face only.

New Zealand's fertile forests with their large trees made it unnecessary for the Maoris to build outrigger or double canoes such as were built elsewhere in Polynesia. Their boats were made from very large, seaworthy tree trunks and ornamented with a boardlike stempost and a high stern board completely covered with continuous spiral patterns rising above a more three-dimensional guardian figure.

Sternpost of a boat, Maori work from New Zealand (detail). Wood, $53^{1}/_{8} \times 22''$. Museum für Völkerkunde, Berlin

Head of an ancestor with tattooing, Maori work from New Zealand. Wood. Koninklijk Instituut voor de Tropen, Amsterdam

Tattooing among the Maoris was restricted to the face and could only be used by nobles. For all that the traditional style was followed faithfully, new personal variations were constantly introduced, with the result that the facial tattoo alone, without any reference to portrait likeness, sufficed to identify just which ancestor an image was meant to depict. We have seen that in the Sepik Valley of New Guinea face painting served the same purpose, but there is no reason to presume a connection between those two regions.

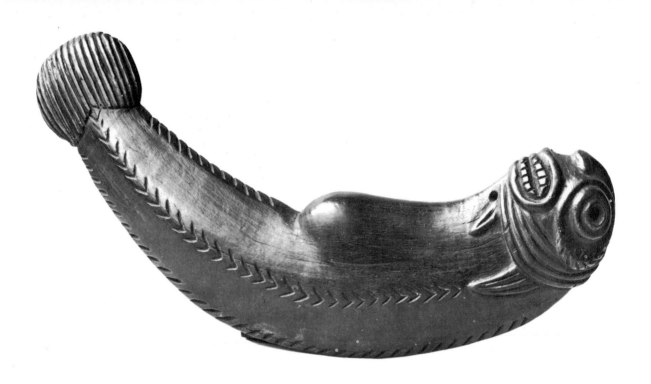

Bird, from Easter Island. Toromiro wood, length
6³/₄″. Museum für Völkerkunde, Berlin (destroyed)

Soon after Easter Island was settled, the other Polynesians appear to have lost interest in that island, which is so poorly endowed by nature. The Easter Islanders themselves found it no longer possible to make proper boats because of the scarcity of wood in their new home, and for a long time the island remained completely isolated. Instead of large religious images in wood, the inhabitants were obliged to hack them out of volcanic rock. Gigantic size took precedence over quality of workmanship in such statues. Eventually, no attempt was made to carve legs, and the statues took the form of colossal busts with arms, something highly exceptional in so-called primitive art. However, native woods and driftwood could be used to make smaller figures, which were more carefully carved. These were associated with ancestor worship, depicting almost skeleton-like beings, or with the bird cult which, here, fully replaced the old cult of the great gods, as is typical in the cultures of isolated islands.

Bibliography

GENERAL WORKS ON PRIMITIVE ART

ADAM, L., *Primitive Art*, 3rd ed., London, 1963

BOAS, F., *Primitive Art*, New York, 1955

CHIPP, H. B., "Formal and Symbolic Factors in the Art Styles of Primitive Cultures," *Journal of Aesthetics*, XIX, 1960

CHRISTENSEN, E. O., *Primitive Art*, New York, 1955

HEYDRICH, M., and FRÖHLICH, W., *Plastik der Primitiven*, Stuttgart, 1954

KUTSCHER, G., *Exotische Masken*, Stuttgart, 1963

MUENSTERBERGER, W., *The Art of Primitive Man*, London and Amsterdam, 1955

VATTER, E., *Religiöse Plastik der Naturvölker*, Frankfurt am Main, 1926

WINGERT, P. S., *Primitive Art, Its Traditions and Styles*, London, 1962

AFRICAN ART

BALLIF, N., *Dancers of God*, London, 1955

BAUMANN, H., and WESTERMANN, D., *Les Peuples et les civilisations de l'Afrique noire*, Paris, 1948

BERNATZIK, H. A., *Afrika*, Innsbruck, 1947, 2 vols.

CATON-THOMPSON, G., *The Zimbabwe Culture*, Oxford, 1931

DARK, P., *Benin Art*, London, 1961

EINSTEIN, C., *Negerplastik*, Munich, 1920

ELISOFON, E., and FAGG, W., *The Sculpture of Africa*, London and New York, 1958

FAGG, W., and LIST, H., *Nigerian Images*, New York, 1963

FAGG, W., and PLASS, M., *African Sculpture*, London, 1964

GERBRANDS, A. A., *Art as an Element of Culture, Especially in Negro Africa*, Leiden, 1957

GERMANN, P., *Die afrikanische Kunst* (Handbuch der Kunstgeschichte, VI), Leipzig, 1929

GLÜCK, J., *Die Goldgewichte von Oberguinea*, Heidelberg, 1937

GOLDWATER, R. U., "Approach to African Sculpture," *Parnassus*, VII, 1935

GOSSET, P., and R., *L'Afrique, les africains*, Paris, 1958–1959, 3 vols.

GRIAULE, M., *Arts of the African Native*, London, 1950

HAILEY, LORD, *An African Survey*, revised ed., London, 1957

HERSKOVITS, M. J., *The Background of African Art*, Denver, 1945

HERSKOVITS, M. J., *Dahomey, An Ancient West African Kingdom*, New York, 1938, 2 vols.

HERSKOVITS, M. J., *The Myth of the Negro Past*, New York, 1941

HIMMELHEBER, H., "Les Masques Bayaka et leurs sculpteurs," *Brousse*, I, 1939

HIMMELHEBER, H., *Negerkunst und Negerkünstler*, Brunswick, 1960

HIMMELHEBER, H., and HIMMELHEBER, U., *Die Dan*, Stuttgart, 1958

HOLAS, B., ed., *The Art of Life*, Lagos, 1955

HOLAS, B., *Cultures matérielles de la Côte d'Ivoire*, Paris, 1960

HOOPER, J. T., and BURLAND, C. A., *The Art of Primitive Peoples*, New York, 1954

JUNOD, H. P., *Bantu Heritage*, Johannesburg, 1938

KJERSMEIER, C., *African Negro Sculpture*, New York, 1948

KJERSMEIER, C., "Bambara-Kunst," *Ymer*, IV, 1932

KJERSMEIER, C., *Centres de style de la sculpture nègre africaine*, Paris and Copenhagen, 1935–1938, 4 vols, reprinted New York, 1967

KOCHNITZKY, L., *Negro Art in the Belgian Congo*, 3rd ed., New York, 1948

L., "Aspects of the Study of African Art," *Phylon*, XIX, 1958

LABOURET, H., *Le Cameroun*, Paris, 1937

LAVACHERY, H., *Statuaire de l'Afrique noire*, Brussels, 1954

LEIRIS, M., *Les Nègres d'Afrique et les arts sculpturaux*, Paris, 1954

LEUZINGER, E., *Africa; The Art of the Negro Peoples*, London and New York, 1960

LOCKE, A., "African Art; Classic Style," *American Magazine of Art*, XXVIII, 1935

LUCAS, J. O., *The Religion of the Yorubas*, Lagos, 1948

LUSCHAN, F. VON, *Die Altertümer von Benin*, Berlin, 1919, 3 vols.

MAES, J., *Aniota-Kifwebe: Les Masques des populations du Congo Belge*, Antwerp, 1924

MAES, J., "L'Ethnologie de l'Afrique centrale et le Musée du Congo Belge," *Africa*, 1934

MURDOCK, G. P., *Africa, Its Peoples and Their Culture History*, New York, 1959

MURRAY, K. C., and FAGG, B. E. B., *An Introduction to the Art of Ife*, Lagos, 1955

PAULME, D., *Les Sculptures de l'Afrique noire*, Paris, 1956

PLASS, M., *African Tribal Sculpture*, Philadelphia, 1956

RADIN, P., and SWEENY, J. J., *African Folktales and Sculpture*, New York, 1952

RATTRAY, R., *Religion and Art in Ashanti*, Oxford, 1927, reprinted 1959

SCHEBESTA, P., "Die Zimbabwe-Kultur in Afrika," *Anthropos*, XXI, 1926

SCHMALENBACH, W., *African Art*, New York, 1950

SEGY, L., *African Sculpture*, New York, 1958

SEGY, L., *African Sculpture Speaks*, New York, 1952

SUMMERS, R., *Zimbabwe; A Rhodesian Mystery*, Johannesburg, 1963

SYDOW, E. VON, *Afrikanische Plastik*, ed. G. Kutscher, Berlin, 1954

TEMPELS, P., *Bantu Philosophy*, Paris, 1959

THIELE, A., *Les Arts de l'Afrique*, Paris, 1963

TROWELL, M., *Classical African Sculpture*, London, 1954, 2nd ed., 1964

TROWELL, M., and WACHSMANN, K. P., *Tribal Crafts of Uganda*, London, 1953

UNDERWOOD, L., *Bronzes of West Africa,* London, 1949

UNDERWOOD, L., *Figures in Wood of West Africa,* London, 1947, reprinted 1964

UNDERWOOD, L., *Masks of West Africa,* London, 1952

VANDENHOUTE, P. J. L., *Classification stylistique du masque Dan et Gueré de la Côte d'Ivoire occidentale* (Mededelingen van het Rijksmuseum voor Volkenkunde, IV), Arnhem, 1948

WINGERT, P. S., *The Sculpture of Negro Africa,* New York, 1951

OCEANIC ART

GENERAL

BODROGI, T., *Oceanian Art,* Budapest, 1959

BÜHLER, A., BARROW, T., and MOUNTFORD, C. P., *Oceania and Australia, The Art of the South Seas,* London and New York, 1962

GREENBIE, S., *The Pacific Triangle,* London, 1921

GUIART, J., *Arts of the South Pacific,* New York, 1963

HOGBIN, H. I., *Peoples of the South-west Pacific,* New York, 1946

LEENHARDT, M., *Folk Arts of Oceania,* New York, 1950

LINTON, R., and WINGERT, P. S., *Arts of the South Seas,* New York, 1946

OLIVER, D., *The Pacific Islands,* Cambridge, Mass., 1952

SHARP, C. A., *Ancient Voyagers in the Pacific,* Harmondsworth, 1957

TISCHNER, H., and HEWICKER, F., *Oceanic Art,* London, 1954

WINGERT, P. S., *Art of the South Pacific Islands,* London, 1953

WINGERT, P. S., *Outline Guide to South Pacific Art,* New York, 1946

MELANESIA, INCLUDING NEW GUINEA

BERNDT, R. M., and RAWLINS, A., "Sepik Art," *Art and Australia,* I, no. 4, 1964

BODROGI, T., "Art in New Guinea: Tago Masks from the Tami Islands," *Acta Ethnographica,* V, 1956

BODROGI, T., "Some Notes on the Ethnography of New Guinea," *Acta Ethnographica,* III, 1953

CHAUVET, S., *Les Arts indigènes en Nouvelle-Guinée,* Paris, 1930

CRANSTONE, B. A. L., *Melanesia. A Short Ethnography,* London, 1961

DAMM, H., "Zeremonialschemel vom Sepik," *Kultur und Rasse* (*Festschrift zum 60. Geburtstag Otto Reche*), Munich, 1939

EMST, P. VAN, *In de Ban der Voorouders,* Amsterdam, 1958

GERBRANDS, A. A., "Kunststijlen in West Nieuw-Guinea," *Indonesië,* IV, 1950–1951

GUIART, J., *Nouvelles-Hébrides,* Paris, 1965

HADDON, A. C., *The Decorative Art of British New Guinea,* Dublin, 1894

HESSE, I., *Die Darstellung der menschlichen Gestalt in Rundskulpturen Neumecklenburgs,* Cologne, 1933

KOOIJMAN, S., *The Art of Lake Sentani,* New York, 1959

KOOIJMAN, S., "Art of Southwestern New Guinea," *Antiquity and Survival,* V, 1956

KOOIJMAN, S., *De Kunst van Nieuw-Guinea,* The Hague, 1955

KRÄMER, A., *Die Malanggane von Tombára,* Munich, 1925

KRÄMER-BANNOW, E., *Bei kunstsinnigen Kannibalen der Südsee,* Berlin, 1916

LUQUET, G.-H., *L'Art néo-calédonien,* Paris, 1926

MEYER, A. B., and PARKINSON, R., *Schnitzereien und Masken vom Bismarck Archipel und Neu Guinea,* Dresden, 1895

NUOFFER, O., *Ahnenfiguren von der Geelvinkbai, Holländisch Neu-Guinea* (Abhandlungen und Berichte des königlichen zoologischen und anthropologisch-ethnographischen Museums zu Dresden, XII, no. 2), 1908

PEEKEL, G., "Die Ahnenbilder von Nord-Neu-Mecklenburg," *Anthropos,* XXI, 1926, XXII, 1927

REICHARD, G. A., *Melanesian Design,* New York, 1933, 2 vols.

RENSELAAR, H. C. VAN, *Asmat,* Amsterdam, n. d.

RYAN, D., "On Discussing Ethnic Art," *Art and Australia,* IV, no. 2, 1966

SMITH, M. W., *The Artist in Tribal Society,* London, 1961

SÖDERSTRÖM, J., and HÖLTKER, G., *Die Figurstühle vom Sepik-Fluss auf Neu-Guinea* (Statens Ethnografiska Museum, Smärre Meddelanden, no. 18), Stockholm, 1941

SPEISER, F., *Ethnographische Materialien aus den Neuen Hebriden und den Banks-Inseln,* Berlin, 1923

SPEISER, F., "Über Kunststile in Melanesien," *Zeitschrift für Ethnologie,* LXVIII, 1936

STEPHAN, E., *Südseekunst,* Berlin, 1907

WILLIAMS, F. E., *Drama of Orokolo,* Oxford, 1940

WILLITSCH, G., "Betrachtungen über die bildende Kunst Melanesiens," *Zeitschrift für Ethnologie,* LXVII, 1935

POLYNESIA AND MICRONESIA

BUCK, P. H., *The Coming of the Maori,* Wellington, 1949, reprinted 1958

BUCK, P. H., "Mangarevan Images," *Ethnologia Cranmorensis,* no. 4, 1939

CHAUVET, S., *L'Île de Pâques,* Paris, 1935

FIRTH, R., *Economics of the New Zealand Maori,* Wellington, 1959

FIRTH, R., "The Maori Carver," *Journal of the Polynesian Society,* XXXIV, 1925

FREUND, P., *Easter Island,* Beechhurst, N. Y., 1947

GREINER, R., *Polynesian Decorative Designs* (Bernice P. Bishop Museum, Honolulu, Bulletin, 7), 1923

HAMILTON, A., *The Art Workmanship of the Maori Race in New Zealand,* Dunedin, 1896

HANDY, W. C., *L'Art des îles Marquises,* Paris, 1938

LARSSEN, K. E., *Fijian Studies* (Ethnografiska Museet, Göteborg, Ethnological Studies, XXV), 1960

LAVACHERY, H., *Île de Pâques,* Paris, 1935

MELVILLE, H., *Typee—A Peep at Polynesian Life during a Four Months' Residence in a Valley of the Marquesas,* New York, 1876

MÉTRAUX, A., *Ethnology of Easter Island* (Bernice P. Bishop Museum, Honolulu, Bulletin, 160), 1940

RIEGL, A., "Neuseeländische Ornamentik," *Mitteilungen der Anthropologischen Gesellschaft,* XX, 1890

SKINNER, H. D., "Evolution of Maori Art," *Journal of the Royal Anthropological Institute of Great Britain and Ireland,* XLVI, 1916

STEINEN, K. VON DEN, *Die Markesaner und ihre Kunst. Studien über die Entwicklung primitiver Südsee-Ornamentik,* Berlin, 1925–1928, 3 vols.

Index

Photo credits: P. Allison, Frogham, p. 176, 177. Zoé Binswanger, Zurich, p. 103. Burton, Tervueren, p. 141. Conzett & Huber (E. Schulthess), Zurich, p. 280–81. D. Darbois, Paris, p. 20. E. Elisofon, New York, p. 18, 26, 28, 32, 53 lower, 66, 71 left, 74, 76, 86, 90 lower, 104, 119, 147 left, 150, 156, 199. Faber & Faber Ltd., (M. Trowell), p. 187, 192. W. Fagg, London, p. 8, 33, 88, 93 right, 110 right, 123, 135, 147 right, 169, 186. R. Flietzge-Salisch, Berlin, p. 216. A. Fréquin, The Hague, p. 38, 40, 49, 55 left, 56, 57, 82, 97, 128, 142, 144, 148, 175, 195. Ernst Hahn, p. 53 upper. R. d'Harnoncourt, New York, p. 126. A. Held, Écublens, p. 22, 23, 24, 30 (2×), 31 (2×), 35 right, 43, 44 lower, 46, 47, 50 lower, 51, 53 lower, 54 lower (2×), 56, 60, 61 lower, 70, 73 left, 77, 79, 81, 84, 105 right, 108, 112, 113, 114 left, 120, 144 left, 152 right, 161 (2×), 164, 165, 171, 178 (2×), 185, 189, 198. Hickey & Robertson, Houston, Texas, p. 45, 83 left. Holle Bildarchiv, Baden-Baden, p. 27, 34, 44, 48, 91, 143, 153 lower, 163, 166, 173, 247, 255. Inforcongo (Goldstein), p. 14. Inforcongo (La Mote), p. 13 upper. Inforcongo (Steppe), p. 6. G. J. Jones, Cambridge, p. 21, 22. J. J. Klejmann, New York, p. 146. Kleinhempel, Hamburg, p. 42 upper. L. Larsen, Copenhagen, p. 69, 75, 109, 129, 130 left. J.-A. Lavaud, Paris, p. 42 lower, 43 upper right, 63, 64, 65, 78, 79, 83 right, 89, 95, 96 left, 140 left, 152 right, 158, 198 middle and right. M. Maesen, Tervueren, p. 23. E. Mandl, Vienna, p. 167 left. P. Moore, New York, p. 41, 61 upper, 67, 68, 105 left, 106, 121. A. Newmann, New York, p. 92 left. K. H. Paulmann, Berlin, p. 39, 73 lower, 111, 116, 127, 133, 139. Schmölz & Ullrich KG., Cologne, p. 209, 210, 211, 220, 221, 230, 238, 244, 246. De Schutter, Antwerp, p. 125. Shell Ltd., London, p. 12. J. Skeel, Ashford, p. 35, 36, 54 upper, 55 right, 59, 62, 71, 99, 107 right, 114 right, 115, 124, 130 right, 131, 138, 143, 167 right, 170, 174, 179, 189, 193, 196, 197, 201. W. Steinkopf, Berlin, p. 217, 225, 235, 236, 237, 239, 248, 249, 252, 253. Uganda Public Relations Office, p. 9, 15. Charles Uht, New York, p. 110 left, 118, 122, 154, 155, 168, 184. Wettstein & Kauf, Zurich, p. 100 left. The authors and publisher would like to thank all those who have helped to make possible the production of this book, particularly the directors of the various museums, the private collectors, and the photographers.